THE INTE

MW01156796

Amit Bhaduri was educated in Calcutta, the Massachusetts Institute of Technology and Cambridge University, from where he received his Ph. D in 1967. Currently professor of economics at Jawaharlal Nehru University, New Delhi, he has held professorial and research positions in many countries, including Austria (Vienna and Linsz University, Institute for Advanced Study, and Academy of Science), Germany (Bremen University, Institute for Advanced Study, Berlin), Italy (Bolognia University), Norway and Sweden (Swedish Collegium for Advanced Study in Social Sciences, Uppsala University, and Trondheim University), and USA (Stanford University). He has served as research advisor and expert on many UN bodies and has been a member of various international commissions, including the European Commission on Unemployment and the Commission on Rural Finance.

Amit Bhaduri has written nearly fifty articles in international journals and three books, *The Economic Structure of Backward Agriculture, Macroeconomics: The Dynamics of Commodity Production,* and *Unconventional Economic Essays.* He is on the editorial board of five technical journals in economics published from Cambridge, the Hague, Karachi, Paris and Rome.

*

Deepak Nayyar was educated at St. Stephen's College, Delhi University and went on to study at Balliol College, Oxford University, where he was a Rhodes scholar. He was, for some time, in the Indian Administrative Service and later served as Economic Advisor in the Ministry of Commerce. More recently, he served as Chief Economic Advisor to the Government of India and Secretary in the Ministry of Finance. Currently professor of economics at Jawaharlal Nehru University, he has taught economics at Oxford University, the University of Sussex and the Indian Institute of Management, Calcutta.

Deepak Nayyar's previous books are *India's Exports and Export Policies, Economic Relations Between Socialist Countries and the Third World, Migration, Remittances and Capital Flows* and *Economic Liberalization in India.* He has also published several articles in professional journals.

THE INTELLIGENT PERSON'S GUIDE TO LIBERALIZATION

AMIT BHADURI

&

DEEPAK NAYYAR

PENGUIN BOOKS

Penguin Books India (P) Ltd., 210, Chiranjiv Tower, 43, Nehru Place, New Delhi 110 019, India
Penguin Books Ltd., 27 Wrights Lane, London W8 5TZ, UK
Penguin Books USA Inc., 375 Hudson Street, New York, NY 10014, USA
Penguin Books Australia Ltd., Ringwood, Victoria, Australia
Penguin Books Canada Ltd., 10 Alcorn Avenue, Suite 300, Toronto, Ontario M4V 3B2, Canada
Penguin Books (NZ) Ltd., 182-190 Wairau Road, Auckland 10, New Zealand

First published by Penguin Books India (P) Ltd. 1996

Copyright © Amit Bhaduri & Deepak Nayyar 1996

10 9 8 7 6 5 4

Typeset in Times Roman by Digital Technologies and Printing Solutions, New Delhi

For
Madhu and Rohini

Contents

Contents

Preface

In 1928, George Bernard Shaw wrote a remarkable book titled *The Intelligent Woman's Guide to Socialism, Capitalism, Sovietism and Fascism*. The book, which was dedicated to his 'intelligent' sister-in-law, Mary Stewart Cholmondley, was not simply a guided tour through various political ideas and 'isms'. It was also an ardent plea for socialism, as Shaw understood it, embedded in democratic political institutions. That was a high point of socialist ideas in their many versions: Fabianism, social democracy, market socialism or Soviet socialism.

Times have changed since then. So has the fashion. As the earth revolves around the sun irrespective of changes in human conditions and institutions, we arrive at another zenith in the political cycle which is the polar opposite. This time, it is the high noon for capitalism, emerging triumphant from its long contest, spanning almost seventy-five years, with Soviet-style socialism. And a new array of political slogans or economic jargon celebrates this victory: globalization, privatization and liberalization.

There are, however, lessons to be learnt from history. With the benefit of hindsight, there is one thing we should not fail to see. Zeniths of political ideas are dangerous. Because nothing causes more suffering to ordinary people than an inflexible political ideology which does not know how to change itself. It tries to recreate society in the image of abstract ideas, instead of permitting an interaction, in the form of a two-way flow, between political theory and social practice. The growing gulf between the two is often bridged, temporarily, by the terror of a dictator. And dictatorships which are driven by an ideology may be that much more dangerous. It is a danger from which neither the 'Left' nor the 'Right' is immune. There are obvious examples. The French Revolution degenerated, quite soon, into a reign of terror. The atrocities of Hitler in Nazi Germany and occupied Europe have few parallels in history. The terror campaign let loose by Stalin's state apparatus in the erstwhile Soviet Union is now well documented.

We think that political ideas and political ideologies must be taken most seriously, because they set the agenda for action and change. But, with equal seriousness, we must learn not to believe blindly in them. Religious metaphysics, like all abstractly held beliefs, must be separated from political ideology. The two do not mix except in a disastrous combination of some form of dictatorship.

We must have the intellectual humility to admit that *we do not know for certain* in matters of economy, polity and society. But this means that we must also have the intellectual arrogance to question all gurus—economic, political and social. This book, we hope, is the product of such intellectual humility and arrogance at the same time.

The reader should know the *raison d'etre* of our endeavour. We decided to write this book in part because the debate on economic liberalization in India increasingly sounds like a dialogue among the deaf. The advocates of liberalization simply reiterate their faith in the magic of the market place. The critics of liberalization tend to see it as an unmitigated disaster. The tragedy is that the debate has little substance insofar as it fails to address the central issues and problems of the Indian economy. Too often, opinions are not even based on concrete evidence. There is, obviously, a market for ideas that cater to popular prejudices. But such ideological posturing is the enemy of understanding.

At this critical juncture in India it is essential to think about the complex set of economic, social and political issues associated with liberalization in a systematic manner rather than be guided by simple faiths for and against it. Instead, the concerned citizen is being deluged by clever slogans of politicians and mystifying jargon of economists. It is time to shift the focus from rhetoric to reality and from dogma to debate. This book, it is hoped, will succeed in doing that.

We are convinced that economics is, and should be, comprehensible to the intelligent person at least insofar as it affects his or her everyday life. For economics may be difficult, but it is not occult. The complexity of economics is partly attributable to the fact that it studies human behaviour in the market or in the wider context of society. And human beings do not behave in predictable ways. However, matters are made worse by the jargon of economists which mystifies the ordinary person. But it is possible to explain complex things in a simple manner. It is perhaps even more important to avoid setting out simple things in a complex manner! In writing this book, we have attempted to simplify, to explain, to communicate and reach out to the non-specialist reader. The object is to promote understanding among concerned citizens, so as to provide them with a basis for making up their own minds in the debate about liberalization.

At the same time, our views on liberalization are set out clearly and explicitly. This is not a book which supports either the over-zealous liberalizers or their equally dogmatic opponents. Neither will find us agreeing with them. The reason is simple. We look upon the design of economic and social policies as essentially iterative experiments. We may know, at best, the broad direction in which we wish to proceed by iteration, but we do not know for certain the ultimate outcome. So, we must be willing to change when things go wrong in the process.

In the book, we repeatedly emphasize the importance of democratic institutions—with the prerequisites of transparency and accountability—because they force 'self-correction', another name for the ability to change when an iterative experiment goes wrong. Governments may be forced to change policies, or governments themselves may be changed by the people. Recent election verdicts from many countries in East Europe provide confirmation. When, in the name of imposing 'market-discipline', the economic liberalizers in the erstwhile socialist countries refused to change in the face of mounting unemployment or growing misery of the people, they themselves were disciplined by the electorate which returned 'reformed communists' to power. The economic experiment of Soviet socialism failed because it had no genuine mechanism for self-correction. Over-zealous liberalizers and right-wing parties may go the same way, ironically for the same reason. Neither learnt that doubt is as important as knowledge in the design of economic and social policy.

Therefore, this book provides no recipe. We outline what, in our best judgement, should be the direction for India's economic development. But this should be viewed as a flexible experiment, where democratic functioning must provide the essential self-correcting device. Since we are willing to doubt conventional wisdom and learn from experience, we do not believe that economic policies should be irreversible. The wrong ones must be reversed with or without liberalization. And we write this book for the intelligent person who realizes that he or she has a right to doubt *any* economic or social experiment and change his or her opinion in the light of new facts.

New Delhi
October 1995

Amit Bhaduri
Deepak Nayyar

Chapter 1

Liberalization : The Said and the Unsaid

I. TWO WORLDS

Imagine the common man or woman in India being asked about the economic problems facing the country. He or she is likely to speak from personal experience and mention a host of problems that make daily existence a continuous trial. There is growing unemployment. Job opportunities are dwindling; in almost every family there is at least one member, if not more, who cannot find employment. In relation to levels of income, prices of the essentials of life are high. Rising food prices mean that proper nutrition is beyond the reach of most families. In the big cities, housing is scarce and rents prohibitively high. There is not enough water. Even breathing clean air is a luxury. In the villages, life is difficult. Living is spartan. Even minimal health care is not available. Education facilities for children are sparse. The list could go on.

India ranks among the poorest countries in the world. Most of the illiterates of the world will be concentrated in this country by the turn of the century. Far too many of our countrymen live without any safe source of drinking water and without any sanitation. Every day, children die, in thousands, of diseases that can be easily prevented or cured. Countless numbers of people go blind every year due to insufficient nutrients in their diet. This poor, populous democracy of enormous size is like a sick giant. It is a country of vast potential. But it is in a sad state. Political rhetoric apart, nobody knows whether this potential will ever be realized in the foreseeable future.

Ordinary people do not know the statistical details about poverty, malnutrition, illiteracy or unemployment that plague this country. Nor do they need to know. They feel it in their bones, so to say, every day.

There is something paradoxical here. For perceptions about economic problems constitute two different worlds. It is very unlikely that an ordinary Indian, even if literate, would think of the financial difficulties of the government as one of the most pressing economic problems facing the country. The external debt of the nation, the internal debt of the government, the size of the budget deficit, the balance of payments situation, the financial losses of public sector enterprises, or the expansion of money supply, are economic abstractions which are somewhat distant from the lives of the people. They are technicalities meant for the mandarins in the Ministry of Finance, the economic commentators in the media and the researchers in academic institutions. Last but not least, these are also the problems which the International Monetary Fund (IMF) and the World Bank never tire of highlighting. Much of the so-called discussion and debate on economic liberalization is conducted in this rarified atmosphere of technicalities, to which the common man has little access.

There is a real danger in this dichotomy of perception between the economic technician and the ordinary person. The daily life of the citizen is affected by economic policies based upon technical considerations which he or she does not understand. This is not particularly healthy for a democracy. But the danger is far more serious. The dichotomy in perception tends to generate a difference in economic priorities which could mean that the government and the people live in different worlds. An economic technician may feel reasonably satisfied that he has managed India's balance of payments situation or resolved the external debt problem. Contrariwise, he may be dissatisfied that the balance of payments situation has become more difficult or that external debt is growing in an explosive manner. But the technician's satisfaction or dissatisfaction hardly touches the immediate daily life of the ordinary person who is looking for better job opportunities for himself, improved health care for his family, more education facilities for his children, lower prices of daily necessities, and so on. For him, these are the criteria for judging economic performance. And it must be said, unambiguously, that he is fundamentally right.

Unless we are able to establish a clear link between the two perceptions—that of the ordinary people and that of the economic technicians, our current architects of liberalization—we run the danger of trying to manipulate public opinion behind a smoke-screen of high-sounding economic technicalities. The technical aspects of the problem have to be understood, but this will happen only when their significance in terms of the daily life of the ordinary people is established. This is no easy task. Economists may pretend, but the link between the range of pressing common problems faced by ordinary people and the technicalities of government finance, budget-making, monetary management, balance of payments, and so on, are far from clear even in theory. In many cases, economic theory does *not* know the precise links. In any case, these links are controversial. This needs to be stated openly, rather than glossed over. An important, if not the only advantage of being an economist, is that you know when other economists are bluffing or claiming too much!

The divergence in perception between the common person and the government economist results in several related problems. The basic one being that the significance of economic problems is seen differently. In the jargon of economists, different 'weights' are

5

attached to the same problem by different persons. For instance, growing internal debt of the government or external debt of the country may be among the most pressing problems for the economist or technocrat in government. However, he is quite happy to live with growing unemployment. It is a problem on which he will organize seminars, draw up programmes and get a minister or two to speak in public, especially before elections. But it is not a problem which is considered pressing by the mandarin in any day to day sense. Had it been the case, we would have seen greater activity on the employment front than on the liberalization agenda. For the common person, however, it is the other way round. Unemployment concerns him, or her, far more than public debt. In other words, economic priorities tend to be different depending upon perceptions.

The problem goes deeper and touches, in some ways, the heart of the liberalization debate. Economic priorities differ not only between the technocrat and the common person, but also among persons belonging to different economic and social classes. The 'common man' is a statistical abstraction in that sense and may exist only in Laxman's cartoons. Much the same is true of the proverbial middle class. Yet, these phrases describe identifiable groups in our society. A middle class person wants a television, a refrigerator, a two-wheeler, a car, an airconditioner, foreign travel and so on. Economic liberalization, which means freer imports or more foreign investment in consumer goods, promises just that. Coca Cola, Kelloggs or McDonald's have become symbols of this aspiration.

We will not adopt a moralist position on this matter. Economic development, everywhere, is about material aspirations of, and better living conditions for, the people. Thus, we will not debunk such initiatives as 'western consumerism' which is seen by some as a sin. Similarly, we are not for 'swadeshi' which appears to some others as a virtue. In our judgement, the issue is different. While

6

better quality consumer goods are highly desirable, we must show a sense of proportion. These are not and cannot be of the highest priority for our society. Better cars are desirable, but surely better buses for our public transport system, which provide comfort to passengers and cause less pollution on the roads, are more so. Cellular phones and better soft-drinks are desirable, but surely better quality ploughs or pump-sets to irrigate dry land and safe drinking water are more so. We could multiply these examples. The point is simple enough: we must know where to put the emphasis so as not to deviate too much from the priorities of the common people of India. But free-market oriented reform which appears to be the theme of economic liberalization in India will not do this automatically. Markets produce goods for which there is enough purchasing power, and since the rich have more purchasing power, we are likely to produce better cars and not better buses, cellular phones and not improved ploughs, more soft drinks and not safer drinking water. It should come as no surprise that private investment, both domestic and foreign, will be attracted precisely to these areas.

II. ECONOMIC AND POLITICAL DEMOCRACY

The essence of the tension between the economics of liberalization and the politics of democracy in India lies here. A move towards a freer market mechanism will give the rich people more power to vote with their money—what economists would describe as purchasing power—in the market place. But our political democracy works on the basis of one-person-one-vote. Since economic reform must learn to respect the democratic system, it has to proceed within this framework. A sensible compromise must be reached between the economic directions which the market sets on the basis of purchasing power and the priorities which our political system sets on the basis of one-person-one-vote. That sensible compromise is both desirable economics and feasible politics in India.

We must be categorical. We have no patience with any politician, bureaucrat, economist, intellectual or journalist who puts all the blame for the ills of the economy on the slow pace of liberalization. He or she understands neither the economics nor the politics of India. The pace of liberalization must slow down precisely when it has little political support from ordinary people. And there is a concerted attempt to by-pass or short-circuit this problem. There are many ways of doing this. The most important method is that the economic decisions of the government are not transparent. The lack of transparency is not simply a matter of corruption, which is, of course, there in large measure. But it is also a disrespect for the economic priorities of the people in the name of technocratic solutions. Any programme of economic liberalization which needs to avoid transparency is not worth having, at least not in the democratic set up of India.

When the economic priorities of the mandarins in government diverge from those of the ordinary people in society, economic trade-offs are distorted and wrong choices are made. Important economic or social objectives are given up, at least partially, in the pursuit of other objectives which a technocrat believes to be more important. For instance, to attract foreign investment in support of the balance of payments and the partial convertibility of the rupee, a government may be willing to accept international patent laws which are detrimental to the priorities set intuitively by many ordinary Indians, who would like cheap medicines as consumers or cheap seeds as farmers. The primary job of ministers, bureaucrats and economists in the government should have been to state the issues involved clearly, so that they could be debated meaningfully in the parliament and among the people. Priorities in development should be the outcome of such informed debates.

In contrast, the debate on economic liberalization in India

generates so little light and so much heat because economic reforms and policy changes are not pursued transparently. Information filters down to the public through scandals with speculation and suspicions about who are accountable : recall the financial scam, Enron, or the moves to privatize the Bailadila iron ore mines. The real issues do not surface and liberalization becomes a matter of political posturing on the part of all concerned rather than a serious debate. It sounds like a dialogue among the deaf. Those in favour simply reiterate their faith in the magic of the market place. Those against it, tend to see it as an unmitigated disaster. The tragedy is that the debate has little substance because it does not crystallize around the main issues or problems facing India.

A particularly unfortunate aspect of such political posturing is the confusion, perhaps deliberate, of economic management with economic development. As we argue in the next chapter, many economic reforms were introduced as a consequence of trying to manage the external debt crisis which almost blew up in the face of the government in 1991. The correct thing to do would have been to separate the objectives of such crisis-management from the long-term development priorities which concern the ordinary people of India. Instead, the architects of economic liberalization pretended that these reforms induced by the needs of immediate crisis-management are also the reforms needed for development. In this, they were certainly encouraged by the IMF and the World Bank. But the critics of reform also missed the main point. The central issue was neither 'national sovereignty' nor 'swadeshi'.

It should be pointed out that even if the government could justifiably take some credit for immediate crisis management, it was intellectually dishonest to try and pass this off as the road to salvation on India's journey to development. We explain in Chapter 3 how narrow interest group politics and the larger, even global, economic forces coincided to create this illusion in India. Chapter 4 cuts through that illusion to document how masquarading the policies of crisis management as the policies of development has begun to retard India's prospects for economic development in the longer run. There is, however, a fundamental political divide on how to initiate and sustain the process of economic development. For the sake of expositional simplicity, we shall label it as the divide between the 'left' and the 'right' view, although times have changed—little is left of the traditional view of the 'left', and the 'right' no longer knows what is right!

Roughly speaking—we may be accused of the error of oversimplification here—the traditional left places a great deal of emphasis on the question of income and wealth distribution in economic development. (It should also be mentioned here that, at the same time, the more radical left—say communists of different hues—tended to underplay the question of the distribution of political power in society. Instead, their ideology encouraged a one-party system in which political power was heavily concentrated, although income and wealth distribution tended to be distinctly more equal, on an average, than in the market-based capitalist economies.) The emphasis on income and wealth distribution carries with it some scepticism about the market mechanism. We have already mentioned the reason. In the market, a rich person has more 'votes' compared to a poor person in terms of purchasing power. The resulting lack of 'economic democracy' in the market place contradicts the basic foundation of 'political democracy' embodied in the principle of one-person-one-vote. For this important reason, among others, successive generations of left-leaning economic thinkers and social philosophers have stressed the role of the State in bringing the ideals of political and economic democracy closer together.

Although this argument is valid in theory, its practical use as a guide to policy is more problematic. It rests on the implicit assumption that the State is capable of playing the role in practice which it is supposed to play in theory. An Indian reader, in particular, would immediately see why this may not be so. The executive organ of the State—the elected government in power—may be high on rhetoric for the poor, but may actually be rather insincere about creating conditions for 'economic democracy'. In other words, the nature of the State may have a class bias which prevents it from playing the desired role. In a parallel vein, others have argued that the State has a corporate interest of its own. Ministers and bureaucrats in government, as also managers of enterprises in the state sector, may be more interested in looking after their own interests than in anything else. In that case, the State would act somewhat like an extremely selfish individual taking decisions and that would certainly not help in improving economic conditions through State intervention.

However, even if the State is not so biased, it may be particularly inefficient in implementing policies. Take a simple example. The poorer commuters in big cities like Delhi or Calcutta have low incomes, hence relatively little purchasing power. Left entirely to the market, the city transport system would cater little to the needs of the poor. The State-run transport system may try to redress this balance. But, for various reasons, it runs most inefficiently. Consequently, enormous subsidies from the government are needed just to cover the losses. Indeed, the subsidy is often so large that it provides a basis for some to argue that the State-run system should be abandoned altogether. This example is simple but it does explain why so many people are wary of government intervention in the market and see virtue in privatization. The more extreme among the right-leaners, who are also the champions of economic liberalization and privatization, believe that most economic problems should be left to the market. And the market, they assert, will find a solution. These ideologues favour the 'minimalist state' and wish to roll back the government wherever possible. This, they believe, will release private initiatives, in various ways, to solve our problems, presumably even the problems of the poor. An almost touchingly naïve example of this is the belief, articulated by the 'right' (and implicitly accepted by some on the 'left') these days in India, that such release of private initiative will bring in large amounts of foreign investment to solve our massive unemployment problem! Even back-of-the-envelope calculations will reveal the absurdity of this supposition. Given the extremely high investment cost of employing one additional person in industry (or in the modern services sector) with internationally competitive technology, more direct foreign investment than the entire amount going to the whole Third World would be needed for something like two more generations to solve India's unemployment problem! Nevertheless, faith is not open to argument, even less to a quantitative evaluation.

The operative crux of the belief of the right-leaners in economic policy is to turn attention away from distributive justice to private initiative for higher and more efficient production. For them, liberalization is a convenient metaphor for relegating distributive considerations to the background, and liberating private initiative from government control for higher production.

III. FROM DOGMA TO DEBATE

The political divide on economic development can thus be reduced, in short-hand form, to a simple dictum : distributive justice produced by the government versus efficient production based on private initiative. In setting out these opposite views, we have simplified a little and caricatured a little. We have done so because it is only such oversimplification that captures the terms of the debate on economic liberalization as it has emerged.

To the less prejudiced eye, the weakness of such political posturings should be evident. In the name of distributive justice, India created a complex web of government controls which became a system of sharing the spoils. In the name of liberating private initiative, the liberalizers encouraged the biggest financial scam in Indian history and may have unleashed a liberalization of corruption. Both sides need to come clean and learn their lessons, rather than go on with posturing.

In this context, there are some, fairly unambiguous, lessons that we can learn from recent history. It is now indisputable that an unbridled economic role for the government in the name of distributive justice is often a recipe for economic disaster in the long run. No socialist command economic system can sustain itself in the longer run. As a result, perhaps, even those who claim to remain socialist today have turned to market-oriented reforms under one name or another. On the other hand, market solutions are often ruthless to the poor. Even more importantly, government failure does not imply that a reliance only on markets will succeed. It is a simple fallacy in logic to claim that if something (State intervention) does not work, its opposite (the free market) must work. This is true only in a dichotomous world of two alternatives. In the world of economic policies, where there are always more than two alternatives, such a view is blatantly false.

It is not only logic but also history that points to the same. The rapid dismantling of government controls does not seem to have helped the economy of Russia or Ukraine, where an economic mafia has taken over many of the commanding heights of the economy. Much of East Europe is still reeling under the excesses of the early enthusiasm for the free market and in many of these countries leftists are being voted back to power. With or without State control, large parts of Sub-Saharan Africa and many countries of Latin America do not seem to have much chance of rapid economic growth or improved economic performance in the near future. There is, thus, no room for dogmatism. This attempt to get away from dogma is also the focus of a more detailed discussion on the role of the State and the market in India in Chapter 5.

13

It is worth repeating that dogmatism is the result of a false binary view of the world of economic policies. Economic policies are more, complex. Some problems can be tackled better by liberalization and private initiative, but others require State action. And, on the whole, a cooperative rather than a conflicting relation between the State and the market seems most fruitful. Therefore, we must learn to differentiate among *types* of economic problems, instead of offering blanket 'solutions' either of the 'left' or of the 'right' variety. Broad lessons of history can be particularly helpful in negotiating over-zealous enthusiasm for either.

Economic history of the recent past has shown that command systems which rely on government intervention *only* have been unworkable. A naïve view of social engineering which claimed that all problems—ranging from agricultural production through power generation to garbage collection or moral standards—can be set right through government intervention and planning has been discredited. To continue to be locked into this mode of thinking is to lose touch with reality. But this recognition must be balanced by the knowledge that there is *no* historical case of successful late industrialization, either in the nineteenth or in the twentieth century, which did not depend upon State support in the form of promotion or protection of domestic industry. It is idle to pretend that the market on its own, with help from multinational corporations seeking profit, can promote industrialization of relatively backward countries such as India. These simplistic beliefs are, at best, historical ignorance and, at worst, intellectual dishonesty or a refusal to face facts.

History, however, is not usually an easy teacher giving unambiguous lessons. Despite their unparalleled political virtues, thorough-going democratic systems have not been particularly conducive to promoting economic development in the early stages of industrialization. To avoid misunderstanding, it should be emphasized that the reverse is not true either. The absence of democracy *per se* has not been a guarantee for economic development. We would like to emphasize this because there is a belief trotted out by some, without any foundation, that dictatorship is conducive to development. But, in some sense, a determined government capable of taking a long-run view of development is important. In other words, governments must change under democracy, but this does not mean that there should be no longer-term view, or vision, of economy, polity and society. The commitment to development, in terms of the economic priorities of the people, must exhibit some continuity and not undergo change each time the government changes. A deeper social consensus about the path of economic development, despite changes of government, seems necessary. This brings us to the important but complex issue of how to combine development with democracy which we deal with in Chapter 6.

The fatal flaw of the command economic system was its lack of any inherent self-correcting mechanism. When economic or political decisions went wrong, pressure did not build up within the system to change policies. Indeed, the market economy embedded in a democratic political system has performed better in the longer run precisely because it has such a self-correcting mechanism. This is why, despite its many faults and defects, the self-correcting mechanism operates time and again to save market-based political democracies from total economic or political collapse.

It only needs to be stressed that the role of this self-correction in the design of any economic reform programme cannot be exaggerated. The economy is like a highly complex evolving organism about which economists, politicians or other decision-makers know relatively little. Mistakes in policy are almost inevitable. A simple analogy is the treatment of a very complicated and poorly understood set of diseases afflicting a single patient at the same time. A good doctor, or even a team of doctors, is likely to make mistakes in understanding the complexity of the particular illness which needs to be cured as soon as possible. Democratic market systems may not provide the best doctor but they ensure that the doctor will be changed if he does not admit his mistake soon enough!

Self-correction, however, can work effectively only if the system is transparent enough to ensure a free flow of information. Fortunately, in India we have a press that is, relatively speaking, both free and critical. But the present or earlier governments (both Congress and non-Congress) in the centre and the states have not appreciated the need for transparency, which is essential for economic development in a democratic framework. Information given to the public has been selective. It has been provided only when it suits the government in power. Or, governments have been forced to part with information by the outbreak of scandals : the financial scam in the Bombay stock exchange, the role of the IMF and the World Bank in the design of policy and, more recently, Enron. The CPM government in West Bengal has not explained why it has suddenly changed its mind about foreign investment in the statement on industrial policy. The BJP has not explained its *volte face* on 'swadeshi' against its earlier enthusiasm for liberalization. Examples could be multiplied indefinitely.

Clearly the success of any set of economic policies for development in India depends, in a critical sense, on transparency of information. This is the only means of ensuring the required open debate in public before decisions are made. It will also force political parties to go on record for or against particular policies. There can be no guarantees in politics on such matters, but political parties may be somewhat constrained in changing their stance if their agreement or disagreement has emerged through open debate. It is only with transparency, based on a free flow of information, that the system would be able to introduce accountability. Reward for success and punishment for failure, which everybody accepts

16

as the principle of a well-functioning market mechanism, must have its counterpart in government.

Transparency is not a politically convenient principle for any political party in power, and none of them in India seem to subscribe to it seriously even when out of power. Yet, information related to charges of corruption, large investment decisions by the government, big contracts with multinational corporations, proposals for the acceptance of international obligations (say on patents), privatization of public sector enterprises and so on, must be provided not only to the parliament and the media but also to the people. There must be a basis for a consensus, or even a dissensus, on long-term strategies for, and objectives of, development, irrespective of periodic electoral changes. In other words, transparency is not just the hall-mark of a mature democracy or a moral right of the electorate. It should become an integral part of economic policy formulation in India. It is, after all, the only means of reconciling the disparate demands, so that there is some commitment on the part of the major political parties, despite differences on strategies or tactics, to a broad pattern of economic development. This is necessary in a democracy where the electoral process will change governments over time.

The irony of India's economic programme for liberalization is also precisely here. Its architects were persuaded by the overwhelming virtues of the 'free market', but chose its worst aspect : false advertising. They did a blitzkrieg of advertising for liberalization, rather than initiating any serious debate on the basis of transparency and free flow of information. Not surprisingly, the result is that the debate about liberalization has become a matter of political posturing without substance. This cannot sustain the basis for long-term economic policy in a democracy. If the economic future looks uncertain, the architects of liberalization have only themselves to blame for the disrespect they have shown towards building the minimum of an economic consensus through transparency, information and debate. They forget that our poor and populous democracy is also remarkably alive.

Chapter 2

Liberalization : A Crisis-driven Response

Chapter 2

Chapter 2

Liberalization: A Crisis beyond Reforms

It has been said that India is a land of a million mutinies. It might be even more appropriate to describe India as a land of a million crises, in the daily lives of its people if not in the economy and society as a whole. For a significant proportion of the population, economic deprivation in the extreme means a day to day crisis of existence. So much so that, after almost fifty years of freedom from colonial rule India is unable to meet the basic needs of hundreds of millions of people who live in poverty. The poor do not even have enough food and clothing, let alone shelter, health care and education. In this context, it may seem paradoxical that a minor crisis in the economy, which was no more than a ripple in the history of independent India, led to dramatic changes in economic policies which have placed economic liberalization at the centre-stage. The story of India's economic liberalization must begin with an understanding of this apparent paradox.

In this chapter, we seek to explain the paradox by providing answers to three inter-related questions. What were the manifestations and the origins of this crisis? What is the content and the rationale of the strategy adopted by the government in response to the crisis? What are the political dimensions of changes that may have been dictated by economic compulsions of crisis-management?

I. THE CRISIS AND ITS ORIGINS

The external debt crisis, which surfaced in early 1991, brought India close to default in meeting its international payments obligations. The balance of payments situation was almost unmanageable. The fear of an acceleration in the rate of inflation loomed large. The underlying fiscal crisis (an imbalance between income and expenditure of the central government) was acute. The factors that led the economy into such a situation were not attributable to any sudden shock beyond our control, such as a series of bad monsoons or a dramatic increase in world oil prices. It was the outcome of persistent mistakes in economic policy that accumulated through the 1980s. Fiscal deficits (the gap between central government spending and receipts), met by borrowing at home, mounted steadily. This was coupled with current account deficits in the balance of payments, which roughly meant that receipts from foreigners, in hard currencies like the US dollar, were less than payments to foreigners. It led to borrowing abroad which grew steadily larger. The internal imbalance in public finance led to a rapid accumulation of internal debt that the government owed to its people. In addition, the external imbalance in the payments situation meant a rapid pile up of external debt that the country owed to foreigners. It needed no great economic calculation or foresight to anticipate that the country was heading for a debt crisis if policies remained unchanged. Yet, the government (Congress for much of the time and non-Congress for a short period) behaved like an ostrich. It hid its head in the sand of economic populism, hoping that the crisis would disappear in this country of miracles.

During the 1980s, the fiscal regime shied away from domestic resource mobilization as direct tax rates were progressively reduced while indirect taxes, which already contributed about three-fourths of total tax revenues, could not be raised much further. There was a justified fear that indirect taxes on commodities would be inflationary insofar as they would be passed on to the consumer. In many cases, they would also be regressive insofar as taxes on essential commodities would place a burden on the poor. The inadequate resource mobilization effort was compounded by a profligate increase in public expenditure. This was attributable to transfer payments in the form of explicit subsidies and unbridled government consumption expenditure, which was driven in part by the competitive politics of populism and in part by the cynical politics of soft options, both common to all political parties and especially prominent as elections draw nearer. It is based on the premise 'may the devil take the hindmost', where the government which assumes office after the elections is the 'victim' of the 'devil'. However, the problem was aggravated by a spending spree on defence, particularly in the second half of the 1980s. According to the International Peace Research Institute at Stockholm, during this period India topped the list of developing countries (including oil-rich countries like Saudi Arabia and Iraq) in defence spending. It is no surprise that total expenditure outpaced revenue receipts. Fiscal deficits grew steadily larger. The internal debt of the government rose from Rs 485 billion (36 per cent of GDP) at the end of 1980-81 to Rs 2,830 billion (54 per cent of GDP) at the end of 1990-91. As a result, between 1980-81 and 1990-91, the interest paid by the government on its debt almost doubled from 10 per cent to 19 per cent of total central government expenditure. With one-fifth of expenditure pre-empted by interest payments on public debt, the government began to feel an acute lack of fiscal flexibility in its expenditure decisions.

These facts are both recognized and emphasized. The problem, however, was more complex than Micawber's equation, for it could not simply be attributed to the difference between the income and the expenditure of the government which was financed by borrowing. In principle, if the real rate of growth of GDP is higher than the real rate of interest on public borrowing, government deficits and public debt can be sustainable. But where the interest rate is higher than the growth rate of GDP, in real terms, the financing of deficits by borrowing leads to an explosive increase in the debt-GDP ratio over time. With more and more pressure to service debt, the government also needs to raise the rate of interest to make it attractive to lenders. The upward drift in the interest rate makes the process increasingly unsustainable. Therefore, the real problem of debt in India was its use in relation to the cost of such borrowing by the government. The difficulties became insurmountable not because the level of expenditure (or even the size of the deficit) was high but because the productivity of expenditure was extremely low in relation to the higher interest rate at which the government borrowed. A large proportion of government expenditure was devoted to consumption. It had no direct productivity and thus yielded no returns. The proportion of government expenditure that was directed to investment, did not earn a rate of return which was, on an average, high enough to finance interest payments on the entire government borrowing.

The root cause of the fiscal crisis, then, was the difference between growth in output and the rate of interest. The fiscal gap widened as government expenditures increasingly fell short of government revenues. The mounting difference between the revenue (non-investment) expenditure and the revenue (tax and non-tax) receipts of the government surfaced as a serious problem. For the central government, the small but consistent revenue surplus of the 1970s was transformed into a revenue deficit that averaged 1.1 per cent of GDP in the first half of the 1980s and 2.6 per cent of GDP in the second half of the 1980s. The unquestioned financing of this revenue deficit meant that borrowing was used to sustain a populist politics by increasing the consumption expenditure of the government which fetched no returns to make repayments. There was also substantial capital expenditure on defence to sustain India's political ego as a regional superpower, which did not fetch any tangible returns, while almost half our population lived in abject poverty. Borrowing was thus used to support expenditure which did not bring any returns to the exchequer. Such a fiscal regime was simply not sustainable for long. It was neither desirable economics nor feasible politics.

The balance of payments crisis was also in the making for quite a while. It was man-made and policy-induced. The liberalization of the trade regime beginning in the late 1970s and the new regime of industrial policies introduced in the mid-1980s, taken together, created incentives for industrialization which encouraged imports disproportionately and increased the import-intensity of production in general. The second half of the 1980s also witnessed a massive surge in expensive imports of weapon systems for the defence sector, much of which was financed by borrowing abroad. During this period, export performance remained modest while the earlier boom in foreign exchange remittances (mostly from Indian workers in the oil-rich Middle East) tapered off. Moreover, our programme of import substitution in the petroleum sector slowed down. The combined effect of all this was that the current account deficit (which provides a rough measure of our borrowing abroad every year) doubled from an annual average of $ 2.3 billion (1.3 per cent of GDP) in the first half of the 1980s to an annual average of $ 5.5 billion (2.2 per cent of GDP) in the second half of the 1980s. This was sustained by a continuous increase in external debt which (excluding short-term debt with a maturity of less than a year and defence debt which was kept confidential by the government) multiplied by more than two-and-a-half in a decade: from $ 23.8 billion at the end of 1980-81 to $ 62.3 billion at the end of 1990-91. If short-term debt and defence debt are included, the increase in external debt would look even more horrendous. Since external debt is contracted in foreign exchange and exports are needed for repayments, which must also be made in foreign exchange, the relation between the two is particularly important. The debt service burden, made up of interest payments and amortization (repayment of the principal in stipulated instalments), also rose from 15 per cent of export earnings in 1980-81 to 30 per cent of export earnings in 1990-91.

It needs emphasis, once again, that the problem was not the borrowing *per se* but its poor use. In principle, such a process of financing development is sustainable if external resources are used to support productive investment rather than consumption. Not so long ago, South Korea demonstrated how this can be achieved. This need not have been impossible for India if the government had been less populist and more responsible. It should have been possible in an ideal world particularly if, for a given level of domestic savings, the government raised the level of investment by an amount equal to the inflow of borrowed external resources. The actual experience in India during the 1980s was very different. External resources were used, in part, as a soft option in lieu of mobilizing domestic resources through taxation. As a matter of fact, the fiscal crunch forced the government to finance not just the import-costs (machinery and imported inputs) which had to be paid for in foreign exchange, but also a good part of the local-costs (wages and domestic inputs) of investment which could have been paid for in rupees, from these foreign inflows. What is more, external resources were also used to support consumption. The most obvious example, perhaps, was the use of short-term borrowing abroad to finance imports of petroleum, fertilizers and edible oils in the period from 1987 to 1989; the alternative would have been to curb imports or run down reserves. It is also possible that medium-term borrowing which provided balance of payments support to sustain import liberalization created avenues for consumption with a high import content, particularly in consumer durables for the rich such as automobiles, entertainment electronics and white goods.

It is clear that the problems of the economy, which reached

crisis proportions in 1991, did not come as a bolt from the blue. The crisis accumulated over several years through negligent policies driven by a short-sighted politics of convenience. We should remember that the economy was able to cope with far more severe oil shocks in 1973 and 1979. Yet the minor oil shock of 1990, which followed the invasion of Kuwait by Iraq, was almost the last straw that broke the camel's back. More important, perhaps, was the uncertain political situation which was superimposed on an economy already under severe strain. A short span of four months, from November 1990 to March 1991, witnessed the fall of two governments. The union budget was not presented, as scheduled, in February 1991. This was followed by a prolonged political interregnum in the run up to the elections which were held in May and June 1991 with the assassination of a former prime minister in the midst of the elections. Taken together, these events led to a sharp erosion of confidence in India among lenders. Credit ratings for India in international capital markets plummeted. Access to international credit lines from private or commercial sources was closed. In retrospect, it is clear that any further deepening of this crisis of confidence, whether it originated in the economy or in the polity, could have unleashed destabilizing expectations to play havoc with an economic situation that was already so fragile.

The vulnerability of the balance of payments was accentuated in the circumstances by two other factors. First, it became exceedingly difficult to roll-over the existing short-term debt which was, by then, in the range of $ 6 billion, that is, about one-tenth of the long-term external debt. The reason was simple : failing international confidence began to pull the shutters down on all credit windows that had earlier been open to India. So much so that some of this debt had to be rolled-over every twenty-four hours and overnight borrowing in international capital markets was as much as $ 2 billion. Second, deposits held by non-resident Indians, where the outstanding amount then was more than $ 10 billion, levelled off in September 1990 as soon as the first signs of a crisis surfaced. There was a modest net outflow of $ 0.3 billion in the period October 1990—March 1991. This turned into a near-avalanche of capital flight. There was a massive net outflow of $ 1 billion in the period April 1991—June 1991. A run on non-resident deposits, similar to what happened in Argentina or Turkey earlier and in Mexico later, was impending. The balance of payments lurched from one liquidity crisis in January 1991 to another in June 1991 'and was tottering on the verge of total collapse. On both occasions, foreign exchange reserves dropped to levels that would not have paid for our imports even for a fortnight.

Thus, India had come within a hair's breadth of default. It could have happened at any time in those perilous six months. And India would have gone the way of many countries in Latin America and Sub-Saharan Africa a decade earlier. It would have been at the total mercy of donors and lenders, who would have claimed their pound of flesh, imposing much harsher conditions after the default. What is more, default would have imposed greater hardship and sacrifice on the people of India in terms of output foregone and unemployment created due to lack of minimal import support. As a result, prices could have shot up in an economy gripped by sudden shortages. In such a situation, even suppliers' credits in international trade transactions (which allow us to settle import bills later) might have dried up. Imports would have had to be paid for, immediately, in hard cash. Transport systems, agricultural output and industrial production would have been disrupted.

With such threatening consequences of default looming large, it was natural to explore all possible means of averting such an outcome. The government, by then, was reduced to its last defences. The use of the first credit tranche and the Compensatory and Contingency Financing Facility (to help meet the increased cost of petroleum imports) at the IMF raised $ 1.8 billion in January

1991. This provided some breathing time, but the relentless pressure of the liquidity crunch was on. Cash margins on imports were raised from a substantial 50 per cent to a whopping 200 per cent. The government used twenty tonnes of gold confiscated from smugglers (which would have been exported sooner or later under the scheme for promoting exports of gold jewellery) to raise $ 200 million in April 1991 from the Union Bank of Switzerland through a sale with a repurchase option. But this was not enough. In July 1991, forty-seven tonnes of gold from the reserve assets of the Reserve Bank of India was shipped to the vaults of the Bank of England in a dramatic bid to raise another $ 405 million from the Bank of England and the Bank of Japan. In a society where only a bankrupt household would mortgage its gold, the image of pawning the family silver was exploited by some who wanted to extract political mileage out of the situation. But the decision to use the idle stocks of gold in vaults was perfectly rational in the context of crisis management. In fact, the significance of pledging the gold went beyond the modest sum of foreign exchange obtained. It was deemed essential as a symbolic gesture that would establish India's commitment to repay its debts in the eyes of international donors and lenders. It might also have helped persuade donor countries to provide emergency bilateral assistance which came mostly from Japan ($ 300 million) but also from Germany ($ 60 million).

In retrospect, it is clear that by mid-1991 the room for manoeuvre to live either on borrowed money or on borrowed time had been completely used up. Options had more or less run out. In terms of short-term macro-management, however, the Congress government which assumed office after the elections in late-June 1991 had little choice but to negotiate a stand-by arrangement with the IMF. The negotiation of a structural adjustment loan with the World Bank was almost a corollary, given the practice of the Bretton Woods institutions to work in tandem in such situations. We must emphasize that India needed the IMF, at the time, not simply as a lender of the last resort to meet the financing need in the balance of payments, but also for its imprimatur to restore international confidence in India's capacity for repayment. Such an underwriting of India by the IMF was also needed to restore access to borrowing abroad from private (non-residents) or commercial (banks) sources in capital markets. This imprimatur, however, came with a high price tag. Every money lender has his rates, and the IMF and the World Bank are far from charitable institutions.

II. RESPONSE AND STRATEGY

In conformity with the orthodox wisdom of the IMF and the World Bank, the government set in motion a process of macro-economic stabilization combined with fiscal adjustment and structural reform. It needs to be stressed that this was nothing new. It replicated broadly the pattern of several developing countries in Latin America and Sub-Saharan Africa in response to the debt crisis in the 1980s. All these countries were under similar IMF programmes of 'stabilization' coupled with World Bank programmes of 'structural adjustment'. These high-sounding words need to be spelt out in plain English, as they constitute a core set of almost common economic policies irrespective of the country and its specific problems.

The meaning of stabilization in economics is much the same as in medicine : just as medical treatment seeks to stabilize the health of a patient in critical condition, economic management attempts to stabilize an economy in deep crisis. Any programme of economic stabilization has two fundamental objectives. Its first aim is to pre-empt a collapse of the balance of payments situation in the short-term by reducing the deficit on current account as much as possible. Its other object is to curb inflation. While the balance of payments and inflation are deemed as problems, unemployment, poverty or economic deprivation—India's million mutinies— receive no more than passing mention in stabilization. The principal instruments for achieving IMF-style stabilization are the fiscal policy of the government (taxation and expenditure in the budget) and the monetary policy of the central bank (interest rates and credit controls). Both instruments are applied as brakes to reduce the level of aggregate demand or purchasing power in the economy, especially by curbing demand emanating from the government. The presumption is that the problems are attributable to government deficits which cause monetary expansion which in turn feeds demand in excess of the available supply of goods and services in the economy, thus fuelling inflation. This compression of demand is often combined with a devaluation of the national currency on the presumption that the prevalent exchange rate is unsustainable and that a cheaper domestic currency will provide an incentive to export combined with a disincentive to import. Devaluation is the standard IMF-World Bank recipe for improving the balance of payments. This package of policies was implemented in India. It provided the rationale for a sharp reduction in the fiscal deficit of the government, the adoption of a tight monetary policy and a substantial devaluation of the rupee in July 1991.

It should be recognized that these are essential components of orthodox stabilization programmes drawn up as part of an arrangement with the IMF. That orthodoxy, however, is based on a set of assumptions which are disputable in terms of economic theory and refutable in terms of actual experience. The optimistic scenario implicit in the IMF view is that the current account deficit would be reduced and inflation would come down, while the economy would adjust at a macro-level through a fall in prices and a rise in output. This outcome, however, seldom materializes under IMF stabilization programmes and the reasons are not far too seek.

It is by no means certain that fiscal austerity and monetary discipline reduce both the current account deficit and the rate of inflation. The matter is simple: reduced fiscal deficits resulting in lower demand need not translate into reduced current account deficits through a corresponding reduction in the demand for imported goods. For instance, the impact of deflation may be largely on non-traded goods and not so much on traded goods. Consequently, reduced domestic demand may not stimulate exports or dampen imports.

The fundamental flaw in the IMF stabilization design, however, lies elsewhere. The reduced demand may simply lead to lower production as the size of the market shrinks. The result would be lower output and falling employment without any sustainable improvement in the balance of payments or on the prices front. It is also important to recall that reducing the size of the deficits alone cannot suffice in the longer run. It is the productive use in relation to the cost of the borrowing (for financing the deficits) that matters. Hence, it is the productivity of investment which is critical as it determines whether or not the real rate of growth is higher than the real interest rate. Contrariwise, a tight monetary policy which combines a credit squeeze with high interest rates may exacerbate the problem both by dampening investment (hence the rate of growth) and by raising the rate of interest.

The mode of macro-economic adjustment is neither as simple nor as certain as IMF orthodoxy pretends. Indeed, it is characterized by all the complexities and uncertainties of the real world. In an economy where wages and prices are rigid and the impact of compressing demand falls mostly on output and employment levels rather than on price levels, the deflation associated with stabilization may lead to a contraction in output rather than a reduction in prices. The projections by the IMF experts and their followers do not prepare us adequately for this. What is more, in the short-run, a devaluation may escalate inflation directly by raising the cost of imports that enter into domestic production or consumption. If money wages do not keep pace with inflation so caused, the consequent cut in real wages may reduce real income leading to a fall in demand and a contraction of output. The outcome, then, may be the worst of both worlds : falling output and rising prices. Economists describe it as stagflation, which is often the unintended outcome of stabilization.

In response to a debt crisis, stabilization, IMF-style, is often combined with adjustment and reform, World Bank-style. Such programmes of structural adjustment are based on policy reform advocated by—and incorporated in conditions imposed by—the IMF and the World Bank. If the essence of stabilization is to compress demand drastically and hope, without much justification, that the reduction in demand will mostly reduce prices rather than output and employment, the essential error of simplification in World Bank type structural adjustment is the almost exclusive concern with the supply side on the assumption that the demand squeeze will not have an adverse affect on the supply response.

The time horizon for adjustment is the medium-term. Structural adjustment and reform seeks to shift resources : (a) from the non-traded goods sector to the traded goods sector and within the latter from import competing activities to export activities; and (b) from the government sector to the private sector. Apart from such reallocation of resources, structural reform seeks to improve resource utilization by : (i) increasing the degree of openness of the economy; and (ii) changing the structure of incentives and institutions in favour of private initiative and against State intervention. The general economic philosophy is to rely more on market forces, dismantle controls as far as possible by relying more on prices, and wind down the public sector in the hope that the vacuum will be filled by the private sector. The underlying presumption is that industrialization based on State intervention leads to inefficient allocation and utilization of economic resources. This simplistic story tends to forget that success at industrialization does not come merely from the allocation and utilization of existing resources at a micro-level. It is as much about mobilization and creation of resources at a macro-level. The emphasis on resource allocation through relative prices and on resource utilization through deregulation and openness is important, but it is heavily biased in its disproportionate emphasis, for it fails to recognize that more liberal policy regimes can allow things to happen but cannot cause them to happen.

In conformity with what has come to be known the world over as the 'Washington Consensus', the Government of India embarked on a wide ranging reform of the policy regime beginning in July 1991. Although it is not possible for us to provide an exhaustive discussion, it is necessary to consider briefly the structural policy changes that came about as a result in relation to (a) the industrial sector, (b) the trade regime, (c) foreign investment, (d) foreign technology, (e) the public sector and (f) the financial sector.

Industrial policy reform has removed barriers to entry for new firms and limits on growth in the size of existing firms. Investment decisions are no longer dependent upon government approval or constrained by State intervention. Industrial licensing has been abolished for all industries, except those specified, irrespective of levels of investment, and the exceptions are few. The law regulating monopolies has been amended to remove the threshold limit of one billion rupees on the assets of large business houses and to eliminate the need for prior approval from the government for capacity expansion, capacity creation, amalgamation, mergers or takeovers on the part of such companies.

The dismantling of the complex regime of controls, particularly in the sphere of investment decisions (commonly known as the licence-permit raj), was both necessary and desirable. However, the removal of barriers to entry and exit is not symmetrical. We cannot turn a blind eye to barriers to exit (retrenchment of workers and closure of firms), particularly in an economy where levels of income are low, levels of unemployment are high and social safety nets are absent. Nor does it follow that deregulation, by itself, will reduce the degree of monopoly and increase the degree of competition among firms. This commonly held view is invalid, because there is nothing automatic about competition. It is possible that deregulation may, in fact, induce what economists call 'rent-seeking behaviour'. In simpler terms, it means a quest on the part of economic actors to appropriate potential economic gains arising from scarcities created by government controls or opportunities created by government policies. Some recent developments in India suggest that acquisitions, mergers or takeovers by firms in the industrial sector have enabled the enlarged corporate entity to capture a preponderant market share. It is possible to cite several examples. There are some that are significant and worth noting : the acquisition of TOMCO by Hindustan Lever; the takeover of Godrej and Boyce by Procter and Gamble; the merger of Parle and Coca Cola; and the tie up between Malhotras and Gillette. In all these cases, the dominant market share so attained in a particular product range has tended to eliminate established competition or pre-empt potential competition. This would simply not be permissible under anti-trust laws in most countries. Given the importance of scale economies in manufacturing, concerns about the concentration of economic power should not become a constraint on growth. But in such situations, the market must be governed either by calibrating competition or by suitable anti-trust legislation. Rhetoric and wishful thinking are no substitutes. In India, the law on monopolies has been diluted to abolish limits on the growth of firms through mergers or acquisition but laws needed to regulate monopolistic, restrictive or unfair trade practices have not been strengthened. In this respect, the present anti-trust legislation is more like a watchdog without teeth. This one-sidedness of the industrial policy reform needs to be recognized.

The object of *trade policy reform* implemented so far in India has been to eliminate discretionary bureaucratic controls mostly on imports, to reduce the protection available to domestic industry, and to bring domestic prices closer to world prices. In conformity with these objectives, there has been a rapid dismantling of quantitative restrictions (quotas) on imports and exports, a substantial reduction in tariffs on imports combined with an abolition of subsidies on exports, and several downward adjustments in the exchange rate which have led to a sizeable depreciation of the rupee. The presumption is that this process (by making exports more attractive and imports more expensive) will shift resources from the production of non-traded goods to the production of traded goods, while exposure to international competition will force domestic firms to become more efficient.

The basic fault of a simple-minded application of trade policy reform in this format—a fault which characterizes the thinking of the IMF and the World Bank as also our Ministry of Finance—is an elementary but commonplace theoretical error in designing policies. It confuses *comparison* (of equilibrium positions) with *change* (from one equilibrium position to another). Real life economic policy must be concerned not merely with comparison but with how to direct the process of change. Thus, even if a reduction in tariffs (or other forms of protection) can, in principle, lead to a more cost-efficient competitive economy, it is not at all clear that the Indian economy can ever achieve this, even after a sufficiently long time. In particular, things can go wrong due to a lack of intelligent demand management in the course of change. As inefficient firms and production units exit, the loss of employment and purchasing power may create further rounds of unemployment and underutilization of capacity even in industries which are not so inefficient. To economists, this is known as the problem of insufficient effective demand. Enthusiasts for trade liberalization ignore this problem of insufficient demand, often compounded by expenditure cuts in the government budget. They claim that 'good products' can always be exported. But internationally competitive 'good products' have to be developed relatively slowly and all countries cannot generate an export surplus at the same time (for every export surplus there must be a matching import surplus somewhere). Again, the process of change, say product development, is confused with the ultimate destination of an internationally competitive economy. The result is confused thinking. Counting on multinational corporations to solve the difficult problem of managing change is like waiting for Godot.

What is more, there are practical problems that arise in the process of change. The economy may not have the flexibility to switch resources, whether labour or capital, as smoothly as orthodoxy believes is possible. And serious problems may arise again in the transition or change. The rapid liberalization of the import regime, which has dismantled import licensing and slashed customs duties across the board except in the sphere of consumer goods, may move the economy from a situation of too much protection to a situation of too little protection and wherever the manufacturing sector is unable to cope with such a rapid transition, the outcome may be policy-induced de-industrialization. Strangely enough, imports have been liberalized in India without establishing a comprehensive system of anti-dumping laws to invoke and to use whenever necessary. Such a system needs not merely a legal framework but a responsive government. If the industrial sector fails to cope with the pace of import liberalization, or the practice of dumping, it may enforce closures of domestic firms rather than efficiency at a micro-level and reduce output and employment at the macro-level.

The process of economic reform is seeking to increase the degree of openness of the economy to integrate it as soon as possible with the global economic system. The endeavour is, therefore, not confined to trade flows. It extends to capital flows and technology flows. Consequently, the *policy regime for foreign investment and foreign technology* has been liberalized at a rapid pace so that prior government approval is now the exception and not the rule. It would seem that the primary objective of the government is to enlarge non-debt-creating foreign capital inflows, while technology-acquisition and market-access appear as secondary objectives. The liberal access to imports of technology is meant to facilitate technology upgradation and enhance international competitiveness in industry.

The approach adopted, however, is oversimplistic. It does not recognize that appropriate policy regimes may be necessary but are by no means sufficient to stimulate inflows of direct foreign investment. The actual inflows into India have been modest. In quantitative terms, they are not an important source of financing even the current account deficit in the balance of payments, let alone investment in the economy. The sectoral composition of direct foreign investment, concentrated mostly in consumer goods to capture the Indian market, is not surprising. Nevertheless, it raises some important issues in the wider context of industrialization and development. These are considered later. Larger issues apart, an almost dangerous obsession with the balance of payments has led the government to extend the liberalization of the policy regime further to portfolio investment (the purchase of shares, debentures or other financial assets in the domestic capital market) on generous terms for foreign institutional investors. It is seldom recognized that this implies convertibility on capital account for such portfolio investment (in as much as the investment and the capital gains are freely repatriable), without any lock-in period (for a minimum duration of time), even before attaining meaningful convertibility on current account. For economists, this is a classic example of putting the cart before the horse, or the 'Mexican vice'. Given the speculation and manipulation that go on in Indian capital markets, this may turn out to be an expensive, even dangerous, method of obtaining foreign capital, for it is not just the dividends but also the capital gains that are repatriable. It could also be a possible source of destabilizing capital outflows, paralleling the recent Mexican experience (of capital flight and massive speculation against the peso). It must also be stressed that such financial flows, which finance current account deficits for a time, may not be transformed into investment in real terms to generate production. This is because such transactions are mostly confined to the secondary market, for repurchase and resale of existing shares or other financial assets, rather than acquisition of new shares in the primary market to finance new investment which would create productive capacities.

Similarly, the approach adopted fails to recognize that imports of technology cannot substitute for domestic technological capabilities. The liberalization of technology imports could lead to a multiplicity of imports by several firms at a point in time and a recurrence of imports by the same firm over a period of time. The discipline of the market would, of course, place some limits on this process, but it is possible that domestic technological capabilities will be stifled. Yet, an economy that industrializes should be able to move on a 'technology trajectory', from importation to absorption and adaptation of technology through diffusion to the stage of innovation, at least in some sectors. In other words, the acquisition of technology through imports must, after a time, be followed by the development of technological capabilities. This cannot happen simply through an open regime for the import of technology with no further vision about the future. It needs the guiding and supportive role of the State, with strategic intervention in calibrating the import regime, providing resources for R&D and evolving procurement policies. Such intervention has been a necessary condition among the latecomers to industrialization, not only in Asia but also elsewhere.

Approaches among countries differ, but the assumption strongly advocated by the government (which is also accepted by some in political parties on the left) that direct foreign investment will transfer technology automatically, is both simplistic and dangerous. Let a few examples suffice. Until the mid-1960s, technology acquisition in Japan was governed by the Foreign Investment Act of 1950, which intended to transfer as much technology as possible with the minimum direct foreign investment. In other words, technology transfer was consciously divorced from direct foreign investment until, in 1967, liberalization measures were introduced permitting Japanese firms to enter freely into technical partnership with foreign firms. But, even then, contracts for technology imports had to be communicated to the Ministry of Finance before their conclusion and also to the Fair Trade Commission enforcing the anti-monopoly legislation. Similarly, South Korea preferred the approach of payments of royalties and fees under formal licensing agreements rather than treating direct foreign investment as the main carrier of technology. In contrast, smaller countries like Hong Kong, Singapore and, to a lesser extent, Taiwan used investment by multinational corporations as the main carrier of technology. This approach also appears to be in favour, at present, in countries such as Malaysia, Thailand and Indonesia. India, it seems, is being guided by wishful thinking rather than any serious analysis and assessment of the best possible technology policy for the country.

In the sphere of *public sector reform*, it would seem that the main objectives of the government are to reduce the activities of the public sector, to facilitate the closure of loss-making units in the public sector, and to ease the burden on the exchequer on account of the public sector. It has been emphasized that the public sector should focus only on those sectors which are strategic and high-technology or constitute an integral part of the essential infrastructure. It has been stated that public sector enterprises which are chronically sick will be referred to the Board of Industrial and Financial Reconstruction, which would decide whether these units can be effectively reconstituted or whether they should simply be closed down. The centre-piece of public sector reform, however, has been disinvestment of government equity upto 20 per cent, subsequently extended to 49 per cent, in selected public sector enterprises. We are told this is an endeavour to impart a commercial orientation to the public sector.

Reforms in the public sector in India are long on words but short on substance. The articulated objectives are limited and inappropriate while their pursuit is half-hearted. The number of industries reserved for the public sector stands reduced but there has beeen no systematic review of the portfolio of public investment that might lead to restructuring or rationalization. There are some hesitant steps, in terms of legislative amendments and administrative arrangements, that may make it possible to close units in the public sector and retrench workers with suitable compensation. Much of this, however, remains in the sphere of intentions, for the political constituencies for such changes have not yet been created. However, the aim of reducing the burden imposed by the public sector on the exchequer is being advertised with zest.

Notwithstanding the rhetoric of restructuring, the dominant motive underlying the sale of government equity in the public sector has been the desire to mobilize resources for the exchequer. This is borne out by facts. The capital receipts from such asset sales, in the range of Rs 25-30 billion per annum, have been digested quietly by the union budgets to reduce the borrowing needs of the government. Thus the fiscal deficit of the central government has been reduced temporarily. However, one-shot asset sales cannot provide a sustainable solution to narrowing the fiscal deficit.

It is also a matter of concern that the modus operandi for the sale of shares of public enterprises is neither transparent nor at arms length. Consequently, suspicions have been aroused about why many of these shares have been sold at prices significantly below their market value and at considerable financial loss to the government. At the same time, non-plan budget support to the public sector, used mainly to finance losses, has been progressively withdrawn and now eliminated. It has obviously reduced government expenditure but done nothing to make such firms viable. The underlying philosophy, it seems, is to follow a politically convenient soft option : to meet the financial needs of the government in the short-run rather than to resolve the problems of viability in the public sector in the medium-term. In sum, even though the long-term interests of the government would be served better by a viable public sector, these are being sacrificed for an utterly short-sighted policy of raising resources through disinvestment in a once-and-for-all manner.

This approach to public sector reform characterized by asset sales and closures constitutes the most unimaginative, perhaps opportunitistic, form of privatization without any attempt at genuine restructuring. It is neither adjustment nor reform. It may imply selling the flag-ships and keeping the tramp-ships, or sending white elephants to the slaughter house, but there is no systematic attempt to address problems of efficiency and productivity in the public sector. The reason for this is not simply the lack of economic imagination on the part of our reformers. There is a deeper malaise which stems from the politics of appropriation and the system of sharing spoils. Many public sector enterprises serve as the cows that are to be milked by the politicians and bureaucrats, including some of the enthusiasts for liberalization. Understandably, they are unwilling to let go. This creates resistance to reducing political and bureaucratic control over the public sector or making it transparently accountable, because it also means surrendering the power of patronage vested in ministers and their favoured civil servants. It is simply not true that the public sector is invariably less efficient. But its severest critics are often those who resist the change when it affects their own power base. We will leave it to the interested reader as a concerned citizen to find out, for himself or herself, how much change and streamlining has taken place, vis-a-vis the public sector, in the government, or for that matter in the headquarters of liberalization : the Ministry of Finance.

The object of *financial sector reform* is stated to be improved profitability of the state-owned commercial banking system and better functioning of the domestic capital market. The architects of liberalization in India seem to be working on the simple-minded presumption that the discipline of market forces will make both the banking system and the capital market more efficient. The reforms in the context of commercial banks seek to improve profitability and restore financial health. The actual and the intended reductions in the statutory liquidity ratio (the minimum percentage of deposits that banks must hold in government securities) and the cash reserve ratio (the minimum proportion of deposits that banks must hold in cash) are meant to ensure that resources made available in the form of bank deposits are not pre-empted by the government but released for the private sector. The complex structure of differential interest rates charged and paid by commercial banks has been simplified and rationalized largely through deregulation. It is hoped that this will reduce the squeeze on the profitability of commercial banks. In a parallel vein, interest rates on long-period government securities have been raised close to the market levels. This is meant to reduce the burden on commercial banks that was implicit in pre-emptive government borrowing. The government has also introduced new guidelines for income recognition, asset classification, provisioning requirements and capital adequacy in the commercial banking system. These accounting practices and prudential norms are expected to conform to international standards within a specified time horizon. The reforms in the capital market seek to finance investment in the private sector and attract foreign portfolio capital. Interest rates in the domestic capital market have been deregulated and the need for prior government approval of the size and price of equity issues in the primary capital market has been dispensed with. It is believed that the capital market will now be disciplined by market forces, while the newly constituted Securities and Exchange Board of India will establish rules and regulations to govern the stock market and its intermediaries.

Financial sector reforms, implemented so far in India, have followed a general economic philosophy of deregulation both by the government and by the Reserve Bank of India. While a restructuring of the financial sector was clearly necessary, this approach based on deregulation almost at any cost has serious limitations. First, the deregulation of interest rates has several unwelcome implications. For one, it will now be difficult to use interest rates as a means of influencing resource allocation in the private sector. This may turn out to be a mistake because the use of interest rates is a strategic method of guiding the allocation of scarce investible resources in a market economy. For another, interest rates on government securities have been raised significantly. This may or may not lead to the development of a secondary market for government securities, which would make government debt marketable, but it will definitely increase the burden of public debt on the exchequer. In an economy where the domestic debt of the government is already large as a proportion of GDP and interest payments already pre-empt a substantial proportion of government expenditure, problems of macro-management are being thoughtlessly aggravated through higher interest rates. Second, the introduction of accounting practices and prudential norms in conformity with international standards is obviously desirable but will require large provisions for non-performing assets in the portfolio of commercial banks. This is bound to erode net worth and will necessitate a larger equity base. Over the past three years, the government has made a provision of Rs 170 billion in the Union Budgets for such recapitalization in the form of new government bonds. In simpler words, the government is borrowing and thus creating a substantial interest burden for itself to recapitalize nationalized banks so that they can, in effect, write-off bad loans! Understandably our reformers failed to make it explicit, but this constitutes as much of a loan waiver as any other. Third, the assumption that market forces, supported by a fledgling Securities and Exchange Board of India, would suffice to discipline the capital market is somewhat heroic where, at least so far, trading malpractices abound, disclosure rules are almost absent and investor protection is slender. There is a clear need to plan the transition with care. Simplistic rhetoric about deregulation and competition will not do. Yet, the government has embarked on deregulation and liberalization in the financial sector without the necessary home-work on either its temporal sequence or its wider implications.

In sum, financial sector reform in India is based on the premise that the commercial banking system and the domestic capital market were over-regulated and under-governed. This presumption is broadly correct. However, the process of reform unfolded so far suggests that deregulation has increased the danger of financial under-governance. The institutional and legal frameworks that will govern the market have not yet been put in place, while the financial market is being deregulated. This asymmetry is fraught with risk. We do not have to wait for yet another round of scandals or scams to surface before reaching this judgement.

For a more complete understanding, it is important to consider not only the sectoral components of structural reform, as we have done so far, but also the reform process as a whole. Such a perspective reveals two glaring shortcomings in the Indian experience. Economic liberalization is about bringing market prices closer to efficiency prices and allowing individuals, households or firms more freedom to make economic decisions. This means a reduced role for the State. More concretely, it means moving away from political or bureaucratic discretion towards market-based uniform rules guided by the price mechanism. But a well-functioning price mechanism requires the institution of a well-functioning market. Markets do not suddenly materialize, but are deliberate acts of the State. Many economic historians have noted a complex interaction between State regulation and the growth of the market as an institution. One of them, Karl Polyani, called it a double-movement: every time the market widened its scope of operation, new regulations by the State were needed to make the market function well. Such double movement is a complex process of adaptive interaction, where both must learn to co-operate. The bravado about free market efficiency and a minimalist State is historically illiterate and lends the wrong perspective to the problems of economic liberalization. There is no thinking, let alone clarity, about this redefined role of the State. This is the first, and most crippling, shortcoming of the liberalization process in India. There is another. The restructuring of economies, if it is to be a success, must not only introduce correctives to eliminate weaknesses but also plan consolidation to build on strengths that emerge from past development experience. It would seem that the reform process in India, based on a standardized blueprint from elsewhere, does not incorporate such learning from the past.

Interestingly enough, what we have just characterized as a shortcoming forms the basis of an opportunistic tirade, against *all* past experience with planning in India, by some zealous enthusiasts of liberalization. In this context, it is important to stress that the origins of the crisis in the economy at the beginning of the 1990s lie essentially in the cavalier macro-management of the economy during the 1980s and not in a misplaced strategy of development since the mid-1950s. Given the complexity of India's development experience, it would be idle to pretend that everything we did was right, but it would be naïve to suggest that everything we did was wrong. It would mean too much of a digression to enter into a discussion of these issues here. Suffice it to say that there were both successes and failures. In a long-term perspective, the most important success was the significant step up in savings, investment and growth, which provided a sharp contrast with the near-stagnation in the colonial era, particularly during the first half of the twentieth century. This was combined with the development of a diversified industrial sector and a sustained expansion in agricultural output which ensured food security, even if it did not lead to a significant reduction in absolute poverty. But there is also the other side of the balance sheet. The most important failure, situated in a long-term perspective, was that this process of growth and development did not improve the living conditions, or the quality of life, for the common people. Persistent poverty and absolute deprivation remained the reality for a very large proportion of our population. The other significant failures were the neglect of human resources, agrarian reform and exports. The declining productivity of investment and the lack of international competitiveness emerged as problems that required a reformulation of policies and a restructuring of the economy.

The failures that persisted in the long-run and the problems that emerged in the medium-term were both a cause for concern, but these alone did not precipitate the crisis which gripped the economy in 1991. They contributed to the million crises in India which mounted steadily but remained quiet and unheard. It might even have been an attempt on the part of the ruling elite to circumvent these problems that shaped the politics of soft options which led to careless borrowing. It was the resulting mismanagement of the economy during the 1980s which, ultimately, culminated in a macro-economic crisis.

III. ECONOMICS AND POLITICS

Economic liberalization in India began on a dramatic note, with sudden and fundamental changes in the strategy of development. In the context of a democracy, it is essential to understand the political foundations of such economic change. There are two obvious questions which spring to mind. First, why did a relatively minor crisis in the economy evoke this response while decades of persistent poverty and mounting unemployment had so little impact? Second, how were such far reaching changes introduced by what was then a minority government (some of which were announced even before it had established its majority in Parliament) while predecessor governments with overwhelming majorities, such as that of Rajiv Gandhi, were unable to do so despite their stated intentions to liberalize ?

These complex political questions seem to have a relatively simple economic answer. The change was dictated by the immediate economic compulsions of crisis-management. The external debt crisis which erupted in 1991 meant that the fear of default hung as the Sword of Damocles. The realization that the outside world was no longer willing to lend to India was combined with a fear that, soon, the people of India may not be willing to lend to their government. There was a sudden realization that governments can and do become insolvent even if countries do not go bankrupt. The problem was accentuated by an international compulsion that came into play at about the same time. The collapse of communism meant that competing ideologies gave way to a dominant ideology, while the collapse of the erstwhile USSR removed the countervailing force, an important prop for India in the past, from the international system. It is not as if there were no other underlying factors. The emerging concerns about efficiency and productivity—even if not about poverty, unemployment and inequality—had led to a debate, and some rethinking about development strategy, through the 1980s. This had permeated vaguely through the political system in as much as the manifesto of every political party for the 1991 elections, across the ideological spectrum, talked about the need for restructuring the economy. But that debate might have continued for some time to come, for many of these concerns belong to the million mutinies we live with. And the law of inertia—the hallmark of economy and polity in India—might have prevailed. There can be little doubt that it was a combination of the reality in the national context and the conjuncture in the international context which provided the impetus for sudden change. Despite later pretensions to the contrary, the change was neither planned nor debated. Instead, the government was driven by the immediate compulsions of an impending sense of crisis in the economy. The response was driven, even dictated, by the crisis. It was not planned.

It is plausible to argue, though impossible to prove, that any other government in office in mid-1991 would have done roughly the same in terms of fire-fighting and crisis-management simply because there was little choice. There was no consensus even in the ruling party, let alone across the political spectrum, about what needed to be done. It was more in the nature of a *fait accompli*. Silence meant neither consent nor acceptance. But there were two supportive factors. For one, there was a consciousness among politicians across parties, which did not necessarily mean an understanding, of the crisis in the economy. For another, the political system was somewhat tired of instability and conflict, so that opposition parties were simply not willing to bring down the government and force yet another round of elections.

In the realm of politics, therefore, economic stabilization had a surprisingly smooth sail. It was recognized as an imperative. And so was an arrangement with the IMF, if India was to avert default. There was, at that time, idle speculation on the part of some and wishful thinking on the part of others that benevolent Third World rulers in distant lands or super-rich, patriotic, non-resident Indians would come to the rescue (and save us from the spectre of default or from the clutches of the IMF). But this was never more than a pie in the sky. What is more, these peddlers of illusions failed to understand that the IMF was not simply a lender of the last resort to bridge the financing need. As we have stressed earlier, its imprimatur was essential for the restoration of international confidence.

An appropriate analogy is, perhaps, that of an army in battle. In the face of defeat, it can either choose to make a tactical withdrawal so that it can recover and rebuild to fight another day, or it can simply retreat in disarray from which there may be no comebacks. The default option, hinted at by some, would have been the equivalent of the latter. The IMF option could, in principle, be the equivalent of the former. As a tactical withdrawal, it could have provided India with breathing time and space to reformulate its policies and restructure the economy in accordance with national priorities and national objectives. But this was not to be.

The real mistake, deliberate or otherwise, was made precisely at this point. There was a confusion between means and ends. The government, very soon, turned the necessity of going to the IMF into a virtue. To continue with the analogy, the tactical withdrawal of an army in defeat came to be propagated as a strategic advance! The stabilization and adjustment programme drawn up with the IMF and the World Bank was flaunted as *our* strategy of development. The most costly aspect of this capitulation to the blueprint designed in Washington DC was that it reduced the degrees of freedom for the government in policy formulation, as it shaped not only priorities but also objectives. It is only natural that the priorities of the multilateral financial institutions, primarily concerned with the repayment capacity of debtor countries, are different from national priorities in developing countries such as India. The economic priorities of the people and the development objectives of the country were forgotten in the process.

The process of economic reform is either strategy-based or crisis-driven. It is clear that the reform process in India did not become strategy-based. It was neither shaped by the economic priorities of the ordinary people, nor did it have a long term view in terms of development objectives. It was crisis-driven. There are relatively few examples of strategy-based reform, except for the success stories among the East Asian countries. Crisis-driven reform is much more common : a crisis in the economy, mostly on account of external debt, provided the impetus in Latin America, Sub-Saharan Africa and South Asia, while the collapse of the political system gave the push in Eastern Europe. The probability of success or failure, experience suggests, is strongly influenced by the economic or political origins of the reform process.

Economic reform that represents a natural transition in the strategy of development emerges from experience and learning within countries. It is, therefore, rooted in social formations and is shaped by political processes that provide the constituencies. Such a reform process can both sustain and succeed, in part because it creates a capacity to face problems of transition. For one, the change is acceptable to polity and society. For another, the speed and the sequence of adjustment can be absorbed by the economy.

Economic reform that is crisis-driven, irrespective of whether the crisis is an external shock or an internal convulsion, is more difficult to sustain and less likely to succeed. The reasons are manifold and complex. But there are some which deserve to be highlighted in the context of India.

First, there is a theoretical fundamentalism in policy

51

formulation which comes to be dominated by outside thinking. This has two negative consequences. For one, responsiveness to changing and evolving situations is significantly reduced as policy prescriptions are characterized by simple-minded analytical absolutisms : if you have a balance of payments problem the answer lies in liberalizing trade, and if you have a fiscal crisis the answer lies in reducing tax rates. For another, sensitivity to social and political realities is sharply eroded as national policies are shaped without reference to the context.

Second, the preoccupation with stabilization in the short-term and adjustment or reform in the medium-term (in the IMF and the World Bank respectively), which is a natural division of labour among the multilateral financial institutions, leads to confusion between tactics and strategies or means and ends in the minds of governments. This often leads to a neglect of the long-term in terms of development objectives, particularly those that cannot be defined in terms of the so-called performance criteria in the sphere of economics or tangible gains in the realm of politics. Yet, economic development in India, or elsewhere, cannot do without a longer time horizon.

Third, during such transitions, for the majority of the people the costs of the reform process surface soon while the benefits remain a distant promise. In the absence of supportive constituencies, if reform is not absorbed by the economy or is not acceptable to the polity, disillusionment sets in and even the necessary and desirable components of reform are discredited. Witness the electoral verdict in country after country in Eastern Europe, where the market, it seems, has met its match.

Fourth, the political and social coalitions which support or oppose reforms determine whether the process would ultimately be sustainable. If the support comes from the rich, the literati and the influential who are vocal and capture most of the benefits, while the opposition comes from the poor and the unorganized who are silent and bear most of the costs, economic liberalization accentuates social divisions and political alienation. The coalitions for and against may, of course, be more complex in their composition but it is the distribution of the benefits and costs, together with their respective size in terms of population, that determines, to a large extent, the fate of reforms. These problems appear more acute in democratic regimes but are not altogether absent in authoritarian regimes. Ultimately, however, it is democracy which can correct excesses: whether the enthusiasm of the free-marketeers for liberalization or the cynical manipulation of the State by the enthusiasts of central-planning. And here lies a glimmer of hope. Liberalization can be reshaped and reoriented by India's democratic process to serve the interests of her people.

Chapter 3

Liberalization: The Hidden Script

Chapter 3

Liberalization: The Hidden Script

Anyone who has read a detective story knows that where there is a crime, there must be a motive. Anyone who is familiar with social anthropology knows that where there is a culture, there is an underlying system of beliefs. A combination of hidden or not-so-hidden personal motives, coupled with a system of shared beliefs in half-baked economic ideas, also characterize the approach to economic reforms and liberalization in India. Like the anthropologist studying the tribe, we need to find that 'hidden script' which the tribe of liberalizers share in common. It is, perhaps, easier to start with the system of beliefs which is articulated in terms of economic theory by the IMF and the World Bank. It is also used conveniently by other powerful global economic players like multinational corporations and international high finance. Globalization is a slogan which reinforces this belief system further.

I. THE BELIEF SYSTEM

As we have already seen, the crisis of 1991 drove the government in power to take immediate steps for the macro-economic stabilization of the economy. The stabilization programme was guided by the economic philosophy of the IMF. It targeted on reducing the twin deficits in government (public) finance and in the current account of the balance of payments. The definitions of concepts such as gross domestic product/gross national product (GDP/GNP) or national income, in economics, make it necessary for the consistency of these definitions to ensure that the deficit in public finance equals exactly the deficit in the current account of the balance of payments, provided the private sector balances its budget exactly, that is, private income equals private expenditure. In simpler words, with the private sector assumed to make both ends meet, the excess spending by the government has to be paid for by excess borrowing from foreigners or from abroad.

Economists, especially those in favour of liberalization, do not often come clean on this point. They seldom make clear that such definitional equality is a mere truism, it is not an explanation. Consider, for example, the statement : 'It rains on a rainy day'. This is a truism. It does not explain why it rains or when rain is to be expected. Similarly, the twin deficit definition does not identify any mechanism by which a reduction in the government deficit will lead to a reduction in the trade deficit or the balance of payments deficit. But the IMF believes that there is such a mechanism. This is a matter of paramount political and economic importance, as we shall see in a moment.

Like most of economic theory, the mechanism must work either through 'prices' or through 'quantities', (or some combination of both). A stark outline of the price-story would be the following : an increase in government spending given its revenue (a higher government deficit) will cause inflation, hence rising prices for goods produced in India. As a result, (at a given exchange rate) people will buy cheaper foreign goods rather than Indian goods which will widen our trade (or balance of payments) deficit. Thus, the size of the trade deficit will increase until it matches the government deficit. In this way, it will restore the definitional truism mentioned above (assuming private sector income and expenditure is throughout in balance). A similar mechanism would also work in the opposite direction. A reduction in the government deficit would correspondingly reduce the trade deficit by making us more price competitive in the world market. This theory can be embellished in many ways with algebraic 'models', statistics or historical anecdotes, but the basic story-line remains. And this is the story-line the IMF advocates, which is shared, almost uncritically, by its admirers in our government or academia.

But there is an alternative story based on quantities or outputs and incomes rather than prices. As the government reduces its expenditure and deficit, the purchasing power in the economy falls, to begin with directly in the government sector, and then indirectly in the private sector for producers and workers who supply to meet the demand from the government. The result is an overall magnified fall in the purchasing power much larger than the original reduction in the government deficit. Economists call it the 'multiplier' mechanism. We think that, in India, it could be something like three times the original reduction in the government deficit. This fall in purchasing power means a shrinking market at home for selling goods, typically leading to loss of income and employment all around. It is this falling income and purchasing power which reduces imports until the trade (or the balance of payments) deficit is reduced again to match the reduced government deficit.

This latter 'income adjustment' story, unlike the former 'price adjustment' story, is not encouraged by the belief system of the IMF and the government mandarins. But that does not make it any less plausible or probable. Indeed, in country after country undergoing IMF-style stabilization in Latin America, Africa, Asia, or East Europe, its plausibility has been established over and over again in recent years. Evidence is now irrefutable that a substantial reduction in the government deficit reduces the trade deficit very significantly through a reduction in the level of economic activity—employment and output—rather than by simply reducing the rate of inflation in the country attempting stabilization. This is the politically awkward economic aspect of pushing too far with attempts to reduce government deficits. It may reduce the trade deficit only at a great social cost by reducing output and employment drastically (via the multiplier mentioned earlier).

The teams from the IMF and the World Bank that visit developing countries, or their home-grown supporters, are not in general particularly subtle or innovative economic theorists. So they go for a number-crunching game based on a whole set of arbitrary (and non-transparent) assumptions which rest fundamentally on the belief that price—rather than quantity—adjustment is the most crucial issue. This they ensure through the convenient assumption that the output fall due to stabilization through deficit reduction would be relatively little. It is almost an exercise in fudging which is not easy to catch. Like the magician putting the rabbit into the hat to take it out again, these assumptions are put in simply to generate convenient numbers, not for their realism but to circumvent the economic and political problems of stabilization. Thus, the 'quantity theory of money'—a particular favourite of the IMF—is used on the assumption that any fall in the quantity of real output is 'exogenous'. Strangely enough, this is a matter of assumption for the IMF and not something determined by how much the reduction in the government deficit would reduce output through depressing (via the multiplier) the purchasing power in the economy!

Unfortunately, it is such intentional negligence of inconvenient economic outcomes which makes reliance on IMF-style stabilization bad economics and bad politics in many situations. But this leads us to the most sensitive questions. Why do the IMF and the World Bank often behave like a bunch of dogmatic fundamentalists, who pretend that they always know the truth?

More importantly, despite the manifest weakness of their economic theory and its results in practice, why do the IMF and the World Bank always manage to find a circle of intellectual collaborators in the developing countries, not simply among bureaucrats and politicians in government but also in academia and the media?

II. FROM THE BELIEF SYSTEM TO THE REWARD SYSTEM

The latter question is perhaps easier to answer, at least at the 'sociological' level. Academic economists find it inconvenient to question the dominant orthodoxy, the so-called 'Washington Consensus', for the simple reason that it is not good for their careers; especially, if they come from the Third World. The international reward system is such that attractive jobs, not only in the IMF or the World Bank, but even prestigious academic appointments, are often far easier to get if one sticks to the narrow virtuous path of conventional wisdom. Much the same is true for the national reward system in developing countries where the patronage of the State is an important source of career development in academia and elsewhere in the system. The world is the oyster for those who conform, but opportunities are few and far between for those who are seen as anti-establishment. This is probably true in most academic disciplines, but it is particularly true in economics because of its close connection with politics.

Journalists in India, in the English language press as well as in the electronic media, commenting on economic affairs are only a step removed from academic economists. Less concerned with the theoretical validity of IMF-style stabilization, one of their main jobs in this respect is to monitor the day-to-day consequences of economic reforms. Facts usually come from the same government whose performance is being monitored to create a bias of selectivity, if not distortion. And, even more importantly, the

61

patronage of the State becomes a stronger factor for career advancement in journalism than in academia. On top of that, there is the inevitable lure of globalization in a poor country. If the typical academic economist aspires to a cushy job, or a consultancy, abroad through a path of least intellectual resistance, there is no reason why a journalist would not be lured by the lucrative prospect of being associated with, say, *The Wall Street Journal, The Financial Times* or even the house journals of the World Bank. Not surprisingly, liberalization gets an exceptionally good press in English but less so in Indian languages.

For bureaucrats in Third World countries, the reward system is even more straightforward. A few years 'on deputation' in the World Bank or the IMF means a sojourn in Washington DC at enormous salaries (compared with what they earn at home) to be followed by untaxable dollar pensions which provide enough money for a secured retired life. For some, this is a mid-career opportunity. For others, it happens just before retirement. Not surprisingly, most civil servants in the Ministry of Finance who have dealt with the World Bank or the IMF in recent times and toed their line meekly or pushed it agressively, have found themselves comfortably on such deputations. The unwritten rule is to push unquestioningly the IMF-World Bank line and be rewarded at an appropriate time.

There is yet another dimension to this phenomenon. Many young economists from the Third World trained in the United States join the World Bank or the IMF as professional staff, repeating more or less mindlessly the received economic orthodoxy of 'stabilization and structural adjustment' verbatim in country after country, while 'on mission', as the path of least resistance to a cushy career. Many even admit this in private. But the story does not end there. Some of them move 'on leave' to the Ministry of Finance, the central bank or other important places in the government in their home countries. With the passage of time and with considerable help from their erstwhile (or continuing) employers in Washington DC, these economists-turned-bureaucrats come to occupy high, sometimes strategic, positions in the governmental system. This makes for an interesting two-way movement. There are some who are on leave from the government working in the World Bank or the IMF and there are others who are on leave from the World Bank or the IMF working in the government. After a time, it becomes impossible to discern who is on leave from where, for these movements are not once-and-for-all. For some of these mandarins, it would seem that there is a revolving door between the Ministry of Finance in New Delhi (or elsewhere in the developing world) and the World Bank or the IMF in Washington DC.

To avoid misunderstanding, it needs to be stressed that this sort of careerism is no less a powerful driving force among the so-called 'left-oriented' economists or bureaucrats. And many of them flourished in the decades of *dirigisme*. For some among them, the career path now happens to be different. For many among them, however, ideology has changed in consonance with the times as they have hitched their careers to the bandwagon of liberalization.

The issue here, at least for us, is not one of morality and, we do not, by any means, wish to suggest that persons subscribing to one kind of political view are necessarily more 'moral' than others. Neither the leftists nor those expounding the cause of 'swadeshi' have any moral superiority over others with a different agenda. The real issue, as we see it, is an intellectual one. As we have repeatedly stressed, economic development is a highly complex and adaptive process, about which little definite knowledge is possible. The problem with a highly biased reward system in economics is that it encourages intellectual conformity rather than critical evaluation and discourages early self-correction when things tend to go wrong. This is dangerous, as we should have learnt by now. The socialist command system failed because it lacked any built-in self-correction mechanism. On the contrary, it suppressed intellectual dissent, and encouraged conformism through generous rewards from the State or the party. For precisely the same reasons, the fate of market fundamentalism without adequate provision for self-correction is going to be no different in India or elsewhere.

And yet, many countries in the Third World reward and promote politicians or ministers who assume the posture of market fundamentalists. These chosen messiahs champion the cause of liberalization without emphasizing the equally necessary need for self-correction in case of mistakes. Some of them have very limited appreciation of the complexity of economic problems, which means a high probability of making wrong decisions. But others have altogether different motivations. Many of them are not politicians with any political constituency at home. They pretend to be 'technocrats', a category which does not quite exist in economics. Their only 'technocracy' is the ability to use the same jargon as the IMF and the World Bank, but their understanding of the economy is no deeper. However, in order to remain in political power, they have to cultivate a 'constituency'. Their constituency is then located and cultivated outside the country, among multilateral financial institutions such as the IMF and the World Bank and even donor governments in the industrialized world. They retain power because other politicians with a domestic constituency are (rightly) afraid of antagonizing those powerful international institutions which support them for mutual advantage. It is only in these terms that we can explain the phenomenon why, in country after country, in Latin America, in Sub-Saharan Africa, in South Asia, as well as in Eastern Europe, economic liberalization is spearheaded by finance ministers, assisted by their leading henchmen, economists or bureaucrats, who share the same characteristics. This is, in practice, the ruling 'Washington Consensus' in many developing countries around the world.

III. THE 'BANKING PRINCIPLE' OF THE IMF AND THE WORLD BANK

This brings us to our other question. What motivates those leading multilateral financial institutions to behave as market fundamentalists? Two obvious reasons play a part. First, intellectual inertia rules these hierarchical, bureaucratic institutions. By and large, endowed with a cadre of economists of rather mediocre abilities, they are handicapped further by their lack of knowledge, let alone understanding of the country they 'advise'. In this situation, preconceived models, routine calculations and the standard economic recipes—which together characterize this intellectual inertia—are only to be expected. Second, as many honest officials of the IMF and the World Bank often make clear, these institutions are primarily 'banking institutions' whose conditions for lending seek to ensure that borrowers can repay their debts. And the usual principles of banking need not always coincide with the objectives of development.

We should know this well, at least after the experience of the recent financial scam in India, associated with the rise of the Harshad Mehtas in Dalal Street. Many banks, with the authorities often turning a blind eye, lent money and lowered their guards to finance a speculative bubble in the stock market. They did so not by accident but by design. Apart from personal corruption which undoubtedly played its part, their lending for speculation was guided by the lure of quick profits (spurred on by government directives about profitability of the banking sector) on the one hand, and the fear of rival banks exploiting the advantage on the other.

The lending and investment operations of banks conform broadly to the 'market principle' and the 'competition rule'. It means that any project, speculative or otherwise—if expected to be sufficiently profitable—should be financed. Since judgement about risks involved differs, the lure of higher profit must be strong in guiding finance. This makes possible even institutional corruption, of systematic adverse selection of risky projects with the lure of higher profits, which goes beyond personal corruption. As a result, banking principles become an unsure guide for economic development. Thus, ecologically unsound projects may be financed by the World Bank and inappropriate technology detrimental to development may be pushed, only if they are deemed sufficiently profitable, so that the banker feels secure with his lending operations. And even risky, speculative projects may be selected if they promise sufficiently high profits, as during a scam or a financial bubble.

Developing countries approaching the the World Bank for loans are often aware of these dangers. Nevertheless, as already mentioned, the international reward system which exercises a strong influence on academics, jornalists, bureaucrats and politicians alike makes critical discussion and transparency extremely difficult. As a matter of fact, India, with its investigative journalism, social activists, and, above all, a genuine multi-party democracy, is one of the few developing countries where debate on these matters is possible and does indeed take place from time to time. In many other developing countries, the population has no other option but to suffer in silence, while the 'sound banking principle' takes over development.

But neither intellectual inertia in the IMF and the World Bank nor overriding adherence to the 'banking principle' explain, in themselves, the massive shift of opinion even within these institutions in favour of a fundamentalist economic philosophy of liberalization. After all, anybody aware of the history of these institutions knows that they were not such mindless proponents of the 'minimalist state' in developing countries during the 1960s or the 1970s. In some ways, the watershed came with the Reagan-Thatcher era, which changed the mode of thinking in the

Western countries and, consequently, in those multilateral financial institutions. The outlook on the relative role of the State and the market underwent a shift of paradigm around that time, as a new conservatism swept the Western world.

IV. THE MULTINATIONAL CORPORATION AND THE NATION STATE

The economic basis of this new conservatism is the particular form which the process of 'globalization' has been steadily acquiring in recent times. The most important dimensions of 'globalization' are three related aspects of economic openness. They are openness to international trade, international investment and international finance in a world integrated far more tightly through improvements in communication technology. However, economic liberalization, IMF-World Bank-style, spans not merely these three dimensions of openness in trade, investment and finance. The IMF-World Bank idea of 'opening up' a developing country goes beyond trade flows, investment flows and financial flows and extends to flows of technology, information and services across national boundaries.

There can be no doubt, however, that trade, investment and finance constitute the cutting edge of globalization. Not all these three aspects of openness have increased with equal or even similar speed. For instance, international trade, as a proportion of total production in the world economy, was quantitatively about as important during the last two decades (1890-1913) of the Gold Standard as it was in the 1980s. The importance of international trade has increased but not so much by historical standards, as is often made out. Similarly, an apparently rigid financial discipline was imposed by the Gold Standard on the monetary sovereignty of nations. Nevertheless, England, somewhat like the United States now, could escape significantly from that discipline, as the dominant financial power of the time. In essence, the story is not very different today from the 'discipline' imposed by the fear of the 'run' on, and possible speculation against a national currency in foreign exchange markets. In short, globalization has changed the world, but not altogether beyond recognition, as is often made out.

However, things have changed dramatically in some respects. The multinational corporations are increasingly organizing production on a global scale. This means that the production process is not just horizontally duplicated but is also vertically divided across countries. Production is becoming far more globalized with different components being produced by different affiliates of the same multinational corporation in different countries. This has some major implications. A multinational firm can increasingly trade products among its different branches located in different countries to its advantage. For example, it buys chemicals or software programmes from one branch in a country to produce 'basic formulations' or canned programmes in the second, and sell the final product as a drug or personal computer software in the third. Such trade among different branches of the same multinational firm, known as intra-firm trade, would appear also in international trade statistics. Nevertheless, it is not quite international trade, but trade managed by the same firm in different countries. This allows the firm to manipulate prices of its products for intra-firm trade, known as 'creative' *transfer pricing* in the jargon of multinationals, to inflate or deflate artificially its profits and losses. The result is they can more easily escape a particular national tax-net to show profit for tax in those countries with the lowest tax rates. At the same time, unlike in earlier times, international trade deficits and surpluses now have a structural component which is managed artifically by trade in components and intermediate products among different foreign affiliates of the same multinational corporation. Estimates are extremely difficult about both the importance of intra-firm trade and tax avoidance through transfer pricing by multinational corporations, but careful estimates suggest that some 40 per cent of world trade in manufacturing is intra-firm trade. The proportion is possibly even higher for world trade in primary commodities. That, of course, is at least in part a legacy of the colonial era.

With branches spread out across different countries of the world, these multinational corporations can also choose, relatively freely, their global investment and employment pattern. Thus, towards the end of the 1980s, only two out of five persons employed by multinational corporations of German origin were in Germany while three out of five persons were employed abroad. Again, a recent study by OECD—the club of 25 most industrialized countries of the world—noted that nearly 37 per cent of its $ 196 billion direct foreign investment in 1990 was outside the OECD, compared to only 14 per cent in 1980.In the same report, however, the OECD finds '. . . little evidence of a shift in manufacturing capacity away from the highly industrialized countries'. This contests the *'delocation'* (and *deindustrialization*) hypothesis : that multinational corporations are gradually moving away from their original homes in the industrialized world in terms of employment, investment and sales. Nevertheless, the fears of delocation and perceptions about tax-sensitivity on the part of multinational corporations are compelling enough in the Western world. It has meant, in simple terms, that the nation-state even in the industrialized countries, is unable to regulate the economic decisions of their multinational corporations. Nevertheless, politically, national governments remain responsible to their electorates for levels of employment, rate of growth and performance of the economy in general. This reality of political responsibility with declining economic control over the multinationals has provided a major impetus to the ideology of economic liberalization in the West. Western national governments now compete with each other in terms of tax-concessions, deregulation and wage-restraint to attract or to retain investment by multinational corporations (many of which probably started as firms of particular national origins at one time). This recognition of the reality and the strategic withdrawal of the nation state is a crucial factor underlying the apparently wide acceptability of the new economic conservatism sweeping the West.

'Left-leaning' economists in the Third World often tend to see 'liberalization' as an encroachment on 'national sovereignty'. And ultra-nationalists try to assert themselves, in the cultural sphere, through the slogan of 'swadeshi'. And yet, they seldom realize that this concern is fairly widely shared in the West. The less skilled section of their population constituting the electoral majority feels increasingly insecure, particularly in countries where levels of unemployment are high, while each national government fears that employment and investment attributable to multinational corporations may 'delocate' from its territory. The implicit strategy is to deregulate and liberalize to entice the multinational corporations. In fact, therefore, we are in an era where the old-fashioned autonomy of the nation state is being eroded by the multinational corporation *everywhere*, both in the First World and in the Third World, but at different speeds. It needs to be said, however, that there is a qualitative difference in the relationship between international capital and the nation state when we compare the industrialized world with the developing world. The nation state in the former has significantly more room for manouevre than the nation state in the latter. What is more, the developing countries, from which very few multinationals ever originate, are at a disadvantage on two counts. They have to compete with advanced industrialized countries in enticing multinationals by offering comparable infrastructural facilities or tax concessions. But they have also to compete among themselves in a competitive bid to lower even further domestic wages, tax holidays, labour discipline and so on to attract multinationals.

Liberalization is the name of this game from which no developing country, 'socialist' China and Vietnam included, wish to be excluded. Governments are thus most reluctant to antagonise multinational corporations on any account. Says Mr Jyoti Basu, long serving CPM Chief Minister of West Bengal, 'In the era of free markets and globalization, no state can remain an island. We have realized this and my government has embarked on a programme of liberalization' [Basu addressing foreign investors in the United States, quoted in *Sunday*, 16-22 July 1995].

V. STRATEGIC NEGOTIATIONS FOR DEVELOPMENT

The label of 'right' or 'left' no longer seems to matter in so far as liberalization is concerned. And yet there are serious issues underlying liberalization which cannot be overlooked either by the 'right' or by the 'left' in a country like India, if politics is not to be dictated entirely by short-term opportunism. First note the obvious. Even more than the 'banking principle' of the IMF and the World Bank, the multinational corporations are in the business of making profits, and not in the business of developing the underdeveloped world. Therefore, unless India can 'use' the multinational corporations for her own development, as much as the multinational corporations would 'use' India for their profit, international investment in India is not going to be conducive to its *own* development. This means strategic negotiation, and a minimal economic determination to negotiate, not to surrender or to give concessions without reciprocity. We would like to illustrate our argument with two concrete examples.

First, multinational corporations are most interested in capturing the Indian market. Unilateral trade liberalization, through tariff reductions across the board, opens the market indiscriminately to all, while we can negotiate better with selective tariff protection on individual commodities. This would protect the Indian market, and that would lure the multinational corporations, while giving us some negotiating power at the same time. The IMF-World Bank recommendation of uniform tariff reduction pursued by the present government surrenders this negotiating power in the name of liberalization without any clear advantage. The basic principle of selective commodity-wise tariff reduction should be reciprocity of benefit from multinational corporations, so that trade policy reform is also used as a strategic negotiating tool to promote national interests. If the United States can use automobile parts in strategic trade negotiations with Japan, surely we should have the courage to try similar negotiating strategies with multinationals. Second, we must give up the dishonest pretension of many 'right' (and now of some 'left') politicians that investment by multinational corporations can solve the basic economic problems of development. For a country of India's size, this was always a day-dream, and now, more than four years since economic liberalization began, India is by no means even a significant receipient of direct foreign investment inflows.

It should be clear that investments by multinational corporations can help, provided these are negotiated properly. But basically we must encourage domestic investment and create the preconditions for development. The physical infrastructure is non-existent in large parts of the country. The infrastructure that does exist in the larger cities is either not enough or functions poorly or both. The legal system is cumbersome. The institutional framework is skeleton. The human infrastructure in terms of an educated, or apportionately trained, labour force is insufficient. Under these circumstances, India cannot attract direct foreign investment, except on murderous terms, in productive activities that have a long-term significance. What she has so far done, is to attract mostly rentiers. These are the non-resident Indians, or foreign entities, who deposit their money at a higher interest rate in India which becomes a burden, rather than a source of strength to the economy. The interest on these deposits has to be paid, but the deposits lie idle without being productively used. There are the foreign institutional investors, mutual funds or pension funds, who bring portfolio investment where both dividends and capital gains are repatriable. Much of this is used to buy blue-chip shares in the secondary capital market. This only means that the ownership of existing income-bearing paper assets change hands, but foreign savings are not transformed into productive new investments. It is important to realize that both these sets of financial flows are also prone to capital flight if international confidence erodes. As we know from the recent Mexican experience, the stability of the exchange rate and the balance of payments are very fragile concepts, so long as we depend primarily on such portfolio investments for foreign exchange reserves.

Unless either the government itself or a domestic capitalist class is encouraged to use these foreign capital inflows for long-term productive investments (in irrigation, in power, in communications, in manufacturing activities, or in commercial acquisition of select new technology) our balance of payments situation may appear to be comfortable and the rupee exchange rate may remain relatively stable, but we will have no signs of economic development. Our priority must be development. We cannot rest content with a superficially healthy exchange rate of the rupee that is supported by expensive or volatile capital inflows.

No doubt, the objection—usually a valid one—can be raised that the government cannot undertake such productive investments efficiently. But the truth must be faced. A government, whether it is in Maharashtra, West Bengal or the Union of India, which cannot run even its infrastructure with a minimum efficiency can scarcely hope to develop some negotiating strength vis-a-vis multinational corporations. It can only expect to lose. It can neither attract foreign investment, nor develop a class of genuine domestic industrialists. Liberalization will not help with any such government in power, irrespective of its political label of 'right' or 'left'. In short, the development of a socio-economic infrastructure which creates pre-conditions for industrial development should also be looked upon as another strategic element of negotiating strength vis-a-vis multinational corporations similar to trade policy. And a government which has no capacity to develop such negotiating strength will liberalize dictated entirely by someone else's terms and not in accordance with its own national interests. Enron, perhaps, is a case in point.

Under these circumstances, the pursuit of national objectives may require the non-acceptance of strict IMF conditionality on the government's deficit, if that is needed for such infrastructural investments. In short, both unilateral trade liberalization and acceptance of arbitrary IMF conditionality on the government deficit amount to crippling further any negotiating power vis-a-vis multinational corporations that a developing country could otherwise try to develop. In this sense, IMF conditions are also tilted in favour of multinational corporations rather than the developing countries.

VI. FINANCE CAPITAL AND THE WORLD ECONOMY

The most determined among the developing countries might, with systematic effort, expect to build at least some limited negotiating strength vis-a-vis multinational corporations in this era of 'globalization of production'. There is, however, another dimension of the contemporary world economy, the 'globalization of finance', which is even more powerful. Since the 'petro-dollar' boom of the mid-1970s, private traders have come to dominate the leading foreign exchange markets of the world : in New York's

Wall Street, in the City of London, in Frankfurt, in Tokyo and in Paris.

Rough estimates (relating to the late 1980s or the early 1990s) put the *daily* transactions in foreign exchange at around one trillion US dollars (one thousand billion = 10^{12}) which is roughly the total foreign exchange reserves held by all the central banks of the major industrialized nations in the OECD. This means that less than a week's transactions in the foreign exchange markets can easily finance the entire volume of world trade for a year. Indeed, most of the foreign exchange transactions (over 90 per cent) in international markets are not related to international trade. They are speculative movements of financing in the ownership of various forms of existing paper assets, somewhat similar to what we see in stock markets. Another measure adjusted for double counting puts the figure of daily foreign exchange transactions at $ 430 billion compared to the United States GNP of $ 22 billion per day and world trade of $ 11 billion per day. This would suggest that international trade accounts for as little as 2.5 per cent of international capital movements!

Pitched against this immense volume of speculative private finance in the foreign exchange markets, even the most powerful industrialized countries are largely helpless. They intervene in the market in the hope of changing the 'sentiment of the market' about a particular currency, but become helpless observers if the market sentiment of the private traders persists even for a few days against the intended effect of the intervention. If intervention in currency markets to manage exchange rates has ceased to be a potent option for the economically powerful countries, it is easy to imagine how pitifully helpless countries like India must be in this respect. For this reason also, the danger of an uncontrolled currency devaluation through speculation against the rupee looms large. This is an open secret of India's liberalization.

The possible speculation against the rupee—unlike against the

75

US dollar, the Deutsche Mark or the Japanese Yen—can precipitate a crisis almost entirely only through a sudden withdrawal of NRI deposits from India which constitute more than 60 per cent of our foreign exchange reserves held by the Reserve Bank of India. One of the fundamental distinctions between 'portfolio investments' in interest-bearing bank deposits or financial assets on the one hand and direct foreign investment in physical assets on the other comes into play precisely here. It has been at the very heart of the role that international 'high finance' has played throughout the history of this century vis-a-vis the economically backward countries at the periphery of capitalism.

During the era of the Gold Standard (1870-1914) before the First World War, 'haute finance'—the network of international banks and financiers—in imperial European powers, particularly Britain, raised money through selling government bonds to organize foreign investment, say for the railways, in distant colonies and peripheral countries. The role of the imperial nation state was to extract concessions for such direct foreign investment in physical capital (say the railways) and in trade (as in China and in the Ottoman Empire) and, whenever necessary, defend these investments through the military might of the imperial power. The nation state worked largely in unison with the high finance of the time under the Gold Standard, until this arrangement broke down with the First World War (1914-18).

The motivation for seeking profits in the developing world has not changed much, but in many other ways the working arrangement between today's high finance—the international banks and financiers—and the nation state is different. The most important difference perhaps is that direct foreign investment in physical assets is undertaken mostly by the multinational corporations and not by the nation states. As already mentioned, globalization of production is eroding the economic authority of the nation state to transfer this decision about direct foreign investment increasingly to the multinational corporations. Thus, today's high finance has to work far more in unison with the multinational corporations than with the nation states. The point often overlooked by theoreticians of the 'left', is that it is no longer the old-fashioned question of national economic sovereignty of a country like India. The stage has changed and the drama of globalization is no longer being played with the nation-states as the main players. While they still remain the main political players, they are no longer the main economic players. The latter role—both in the globalization of production and in the globalization of finance—has been taken over by the multinational corporations and the private international banking or financial institutions. They must be recognized as the two decisive players in the world economy vis-a-vis whom negotiating strategies need to be formulated. The major economic and political implications of this changed reality, for developing countries, should be emphasized if we wish to maximize India's economic room for manouevre in this era of globalization.

To put the matter schematically in another way, there is a separation of decision-making on the types of investment. For our professional economist readers, this is analogous to the Keynesian separation between 'investment' and 'savings'. In simpler terms, 'high finance' decides on the pattern of global accumulation of portfolio investments (and the pattern of wealth holding in secondary markets) in financial assets, while multinational corporations decide on the pattern of global investments in physical capital assets, whether in infrastructure or in factories. In today's world, the two sets of decisions are largely separated. Even on its own terms, all political considerations apart, successful economic liberalization by some developing countries such as Singapore and Hong Kong, basically rests on their ability to bridge this separation of decisions between high finance and multinational corporations. India's liberalization has failed almost entirely so far in this respect.

VII. TRAPS AND CORRECTIVES

The fact that India has failed miserably since its economic liberalization began has many symptoms. Its clearest symptom is the growing accumulation of foreign-held financial or portfolio investments and deposits and, despite a lot of self-congratulation by the Ministry of Finance, an extreme lack of interest by multinational corporations to invest in physical capital in India. Consequently, India's economic policy has been trapped into paying much higher than international (after-tax) interest rates to attract and retain these financial investments in India in rupee-denominated assets. But the high interest rates have also discouraged investors, particularly domestic firms, from physical capital accumulation. The first sad paradox of India's economic liberalization, in contrast to other successful cases such as Japan or South Korea, has been to discourage domestic investors for the illusory gain of a comfortable balance of payments situation or a stable and strong rupee. The show has been kept going so far by attracting rentiers to hold portfolio investments in India, but real capital formation in India has also been discouraged by the very same policies. It must be said categorically that, if these trends continue, our economic future is grim. If these policies continue to be pursued, it will trap us more and more in a high-interest rate economy meant to serve the cause of rentiers abroad without economic dynamism or growth at home.

The international 'debt crisis' erupting from time to time—in Mexico, in Brazil, in Argentina, in Sub-Saharan Africa, or in India—is a recurring manifestation of this very phenomenon. Both economic calculations and common sense would suggest that if portfolio investment from rentiers can be utilized sufficiently productively to generate a growth rate of GDP high enough to exceed the (real) interest rate, even a large and growing debt need not precipitate a crisis. The point is, how productively can we utilize what we borrow, not how much we borrow. This is equally true of what the government borrows at home or abroad.

The intellectual inertia of the orthodox economics of the IMF and the World Bank (comparable in many ways to the rigidities of orthodox Marxism!), combined with their self-interests as predominantly banking institutions, encourages them often to recommend a set of simplistic policies which strengthen this trap of economic stagnation, rather than imparting dynamism in development. They talk of governmental austerity in finance, without identifying the obvious : the reasons for the poor utilization or the low productivity of government and private investment. Instead, they pretend that private investment is always productive and government investment is never productive.. Similarly, a government deficit is always considered bad, irrespective of the use for which the government borrows. And yet the obvious must be faced : political patronage and corruption, which require the white elephants of the public sector, are the two main problems that make difficult the productive utilization of government revenue. It is not public expenditure per se but the constraints on its productive use in terms of political patronage and corruption that must be criticized. Perhaps, the only way to face this problem is by strengthening domestic competition and emphasising transparency in decision-making. Instead, the present government has pursued opposite policies : inviting foreign investment on terms detrimental to domestic competition, often without competitive bidding or open tenders. Enron has become the political symbol of this failure, and the responsibility for total lack of transparency surrounding that decision must be shared by the central government and the state government in power at that time.

But the same argument must apply also to our domestic white elephants in the public sector and in the private sector. The 'open sky' policy is an example. Wider competition on the basis of open tenders for domestic producers and freer access to information would do a lot to curb the political patronage which makes investment unproductive. Similarly, stopping the transfer of money in the name of 'industrial sickness' to private industrialists would keep political patronage in check; instead white papers by experts from outside the government and industry, with workers, and managers' representation, would make transparent the basis of the sickness. This is the kind of liberalization India needs. Simply mouthing the word 'privatization' as in a tired gramophone record is no solution. We repeat that private bidders from inside the country can come forward only if the current high interest rate policy, which satisfies rentiers, is abandoned while, at the same time, the public sector corporations also take part in the bidding on a transparent basis. This is where competition must begin, and the government has a responsibility in setting these conditions right.

One of the most sensitive political issues in achieving transparency is the surrendering of the power of political patronage. A dramatic example is larger pro-poor expenditure before elections, or a higher tolerance for government deficits by the same liberalizers. Lack of transparency is also helped by the mystique of defence spending. Our politicians—'left' and 'right' alike—will have to understand clearly that India's defence strength will not depend on jeopardizing transparency in the name of 'military secrets', and importing secretly from abroad with high possibilities of corruption or of kick-backs. Transparency everywhere should be the overriding principle, with all defence spending, by and large, subject to the same rule.

The IMF and the World Bank are also eloquent on the virtues of achieving transparency through curbing bureaucratic discretionary decisions and imposing general (price-based) rules. For example, a uniform tariff rate visible to everyone rather than a discretionary quota system to regulate imports is rightly justified on this basis. Similarly, a general high interest rate policy rather than selective credit rationing could be justified. The generalized economic argument is that scarce goods or resources should be distributed through transparent prices in the market rather than opaque quantity controls of the government. Both the IMF and the World Bank, in their general mistrust of the economic role of governments, strongly advocate rules rather than discretion, as the debate is known among economists. And yet, is it not surprising that they say nothing, and do not themselves behave transparently, when something like Enron comes to light? Certainly, it was the clearest case of wrong bureaucratic discretion encouraged by the same politicians who have embraced the cause of liberalization in India. As the World Bank objected to the deal earlier, should these objections not have been made public?

It is a popular over-simplification to say that the IMF and the World Bank work in unison with the multinational corporations in developing countries. In some ways, the truth is even more pathetic than that. These multilateral financial institutions are largely helpless in directing productive direct investment by multinational corporations to a country, even when the country succeeds in attracting some financial portfolio investment. India today is a case in point. So the IMF and the World Bank pretend that more and more economic and political concessions to direct foreign investment are needed to do the trick. This not only puts developing countries in a hopeless competition to attract foreign investment but is usually counter-productive. Direct foreign investment will come to India only if, on the demand side, the Indian market is expanding with a stable political framework; and, on the supply side, large public investments in infrastructure and skill formation reduce costs. And, at the same time, direct foreign investment will be forced to serve rather than fleece the country, if they face acute domestic and foreign competition for efficiency. None of this is even thinkable without transparency in the economic system, just as it is not possible if the government manipulates economic rules in the name of discretion to suit its own purpose.

In particular, the soft-option of simply offering concessions to corporations will not work. Sub-Saharan Africa and some of the least developed parts of Latin America would have had in that case the lion's share of direct foreign investment in the world economy. Instead, it flows mostly to the OECD (68 per cent) or now to East and South-East Asia (15 per cent), precisely because success breeds success as the fundamental rule. A fast growing economy, with or without strong government regulation, and a stable socio-political environment is necessary for this. The austerity measures of the IMF may help their own banking interests, and even our balance of payments, but will not create that necessary climate for foreign investment which would produce goods and services. The central and the state governments can achieve this only by functioning well, undertaking public investment when necessary and behaving transparently. Thus, irrespective of the political label of the 'right' or the 'left', and notwithstanding the personal vested interests of economists, bureaucrats and politicians, genuine liberalization for development begins from transparency of negotiations. The interests of the country, in our case India, must be stated clearly while the size of the domestic market and domestic industrial strength must be enhanced through active government action including protection and government spending (if necessary through a deficit). This would provide negotiating strength in terms of both the carrot (domestic market) and the stick (domestic competitors). Only then can investments by multinational corporations play an important supplementary role in our development. Otherwise, it will remain a self-serving bluff, to serve the interests of a handful rather than the interests of the country.

Chapter 4

Liberalization : What Does it Mean for
Development?

The mood of the moment, among those who make decisions and shape opinions in India, is such that economic liberalization is perceived as both virtue and necessity. But to the citizen it is obvious that economic liberalization is no panacea. And only the dishonest or the naïve can think of it as a magic wand. Intellectual honesty requires a candid assessment of economic liberalization in India, not in the abstract but with concrete reference to India's problems, priorities and objectives.

This chapter attempts such an assessment. In doing so, it asks, and endeavours to answer, three questions. Has economic liberalization, which was crisis-driven, provided a sustainable solution to the pressing problems in the management of the economy? Does economic liberalization, as conceived, address the people's economic priorities? Is the design of economic liberalization consistent with the long term objectives of development?

The first question, which represents the concerns of the government, has received much of the attention. The second question, which reflects the interests of the common people, has come up but received relatively little systematic attention. The third question, which is about a shared vision of the evolution of economy and society is seldom raised. It is particularly important to redress the balance because the debate on economic liberalization in India tends to focus on what is said and neglects what remains unsaid. A more complete assessment cannot stop with errors of commission. It must also address errors of omission.

I. ECONOMIC PROBLEMS OF THE GOVERNMENT

We have shown that problems faced by the government in the management of the economy, which assumed crisis proportions in 1991, dictated a programme of stabilization, adjustment and economic reform. The immediate short-term compulsions were managing the balance of payments situation (to overcome the external debt crisis) and restraining inflation. The medium-term needs were finding a sustainable solution to the fiscal crisis and returning the economy to a path of sustained growth (in part through an increase in the productivity of investment). Does the actual experience since then suggest that liberalization has resolved these problems? Let us consider them in turn.

External Sector

The balance of payments situation, it would seem, has been transformed. The capital flight from repatriable deposits held by non-resident Indians, which was threateningly large during the first half of 1991-92, came to a stop. The exposure in terms of short-term external debt, which became increasingly difficult to roll-over and could have been called in by lenders for liquidation at any time during the external debt crisis, has been substantially reduced. Most important, perhaps, the level of foreign exchange reserves climbed from a meagre $ 2.2 billion in end-March 1991 to $ 6.4 billion in end-March 1993 and $ 20.8 billion in end-March 1995. It is this story of rags to riches in the external sector which is emphasized by the government and seen as the biggest feather in the cap of liberalization. The turn-around should indeed be rated as a success provided the underlying factors are sustainable.

The adjustment in the balance of payments, during the period from 1991-92 to 1994-95, was based on a substantial reduction in the balance of trade deficit. Much of this adjustment, however, was attributable to import contraction rather than export expansion. The sluggishness of import demand was such that the dollar value of total imports (as also non oil-imports) remained lower than it was in 1990-91 for three years and exceeded that level only in 1994-95. Export performance, which was poor for the first two years, made a contribution in 1993-94 and 1994-95 as the dollar value of exports registered an impressive growth. It needs to be stressed that the process of stabilization will not be complete unless the export surge is maintained and the balance of trade situation improves even after import demand revives with growth in the economy.

The smaller trade deficits also meant smaller current account deficits. This reduced the overall financing need (net payments due in foreign exchange), which, combined with capital inflows, was responsible for the build-up of reserves. But financing was not available from the usual sources such as external assistance, where net resource inflows continued to decline, or commercial borrowing, where access to international capital markets was virtually closed. During this period from 1991-92 to 1993-94, there were three main sources of external finance. The first set was constituted by borrowing from the IMF, structural adjustment loans from the World Bank or the Asian Development Bank and special bilateral assistance from donor countries. Such exceptional financing provided $ 5.8 billion in the period from 1991-92 to 1993-94. The second set was made up of capital flows that originated in non-residents induced by amnesties (where no questions were asked about the sources of foreign exchange) and special deposits (which offered more attractive terms than elsewhere). Taken together, these yielded $ 5.6 billion in the period from 1991-92 to 1993-94. The third set comprised private foreign capital inflows, in which direct foreign investment was not new but portfolio investment was altogether new. Direct investment added up to a meagre $ 1 billion in the period from 1991-92 to 1993-94, while portfolio investment was $ 3.5 billion in 1993-94 alone.

It is clear that the extraordinary capital flows in the form of borrowing from multilateral financial institutions, or from non-residents, are once-and-for-all in nature and cannot provide a sustained access to external resources. What is more, much of this was in essence borrowing abroad to support the balance of payments, which led to a rapid accumulation of external debt. Consequently, between end-March 1991 and end-March 1994, the outstanding external debt (excluding short-term debt and rupee-debt) increased from $ 62.4 billion to $ 76.9 billion (this figure is estimated at $ 81.5 billion in end-March 1995). Although foreign investment represented non-debt-creating capital flows, the share of direct investment was small while that of portfolio investment was large. Recent experience from elsewhere, particularly of Mexico, highlights the vulnerability of relying on such portfolio investment inflows insofar as they are extremely sensitive to the 'climate of confidence' created for these investors. In effect, this means that economic policies of the government must be far more sensitive to the perceptions of portfolio investors than to the needs of the economy or the priorities of the people. This is the trap the Indian economy is moving into.

In this context, it is worth noting that the comfort implicit in the size of reserves may be more illusory than real. These foreign currency assets are more than matched by foreign exchange liabilities which have short maturities or can be withdrawn on demand. This is the 'maturity mismatch' problem underlying many liquidity crises around the world. Consider, for example, the situation in India at the end of March 1995. The level of foreign exchange reserves was $ 20.8 billion. Short-term debt with a maturity of six months, or less, was $ 2 billion. Short-term debt with a maturity of more than six months, upto one year, was another $ 2.3 billion. The par value of outstanding portfolio investment, without allowing for capital gains realizable and repatriable, was $ 7.1 billion. These short-term liabilities in foreign exchange added up to a massive $ 11.4 billion, which was more than 50 per cent of foreign exchange reserves. But that is not all. The outstanding stock of repatriable deposits held in India, mostly by non-residents but partly by foreign entities, with a maturity of more than one year and upto three years, was as much as $ 12.4 billion. It must be recognized that such deposits can be withdrawn on demand. Recent experience in India with such deposits, and in Mexico with portfolio investment, confirms that these inflows are susceptible to capital flight at the hint of any crisis of confidence. Thus, at the end of the fiscal year 1994-95, the total liabilities in foreign exchange, which could be called in at short notice, were $ 23.8 billion compared with reserves of $ 20.8 billion. Are we really doing that well in managing our balance of payments or creating confidence in our currency ?

Inflation

The euphoria about the management of the external sector is not matched by a confidence about the control of inflation, even among the enthusiasts for liberalization.

It is necessary to begin with a primer about the ways in which inflation is measured. This understanding is needed because governments everywhere are prone to juggling statistics and obfuscating facts. In India, annual rates of inflation are measured in terms of the wholesale price index or the consumer price indices for different socio-economic groups like industrial workers, urban non-manual employees and agricultural labourers. The wholesale price index covers all commodities whereas the consumer price indices are limited to representative consumption baskets for the specified consumer group. Thus, the measure of inflation depends upon the price index, since the mix of commodities and the relative importance or weight of each commodity in the expenditure budget differs among consumers of different groups. But that is not all. It is possible to measure inflation either on a point-to-point basis or on an average-of-period basis. Point-to-point rates of inflation compare the price level on the last day of a fiscal year (or any specified day in the year) with the price level on the last day of the preceding fiscal year (or the corresponding day in the preceding year). Average-of-period rates of inflation compare the average price level during the 52 weeks of a fiscal year (or any 52-week period) with the average price level during the 52 weeks of the preceding fiscal year (or the preceding 52-week period). It is a matter of arithmetic that point-to-point rates are higher than average-of-period rates when there is an acceleration in the rate of inflation and lower when there is a deceleration in the rates of inflation.

Given that inflation is a sensitive political issue, governments in power tend to use different price indices and emphasize different rates at different times according to their convenience. The irony is that the woman in the household or the man in the street is not concerned with rates of inflation. In the mind of an average person, there is a 'price perception index' which is based on prices paid. This judgement cannot be clouded by statistical jugglery. Newspapers may report that the rate of inflation has come down this week, this month or this year. For the ordinary person, what matters is that prices are higher than they were last week, last month or last year. This price perception index has two dimensions. The first is that the consumer is concerned about the proportionate increase in prices over a period of time : the rate of inflation may be 10 per cent per annum but it means that anything which could be bought in the market for Rs 100 five years ago now costs Rs'

161. The second is that the consumer is worried about the absolute price level in relation to his or her money income: the price of rice has increased from Rs 5 per kg to Rs 10 per kg (100 per cent), of wheat from Rs 2 per kg to Rs 4 per kg (100 per cent), of sugar from Rs 8 per kg to Rs 15 per kg (almost 100 per cent), or of edible oils (mustard and groundnut) from the range of Rs 20-25 per kg to the range of Rs 40-50 per kg (100 per cent); while money income increased from, say, Rs 2000 to Rs 3000 per month (only 50 per cent).

The evidence available for the period since 1991 suggests far from a turn-around in inflation. To cut a long story short, inflation remained in the range of 10 per cent per annum irrespective of how we measure it. This can be described as a success only if Latin American economies are our point of reference. It is close to a failure of liberalization in combating inflation if India's past record is taken as the norm. Indeed, the quinquennium from 1990-91 to 1994-95 is the longest period of sustained double-digit inflation in independent India. This persistent inflation during the first half of the 1990s is particularly worrisome for the liberalizers. For one, it has coincided, for most of the time, with a concerted attempt at stabilization, the stated objective of which is to bring down inflation. For another, it has coincided, entirely, with five good monsoons in a row. What is more, the economy has not witnessed any significant exogenous shock, such as a jump in oil prices, during this period.

We must look for an explanation. The government claims that its stabilization policies have played a leading role in arresting inflation. It is not clear how. In principle, fiscal austerity and monetary discipline, which imposed a cost on the economy in terms of higher unemployment and slower growth through a contraction of aggregate demand, should have also dampened inflation propelled by excess demand. However, the potency of this policy may have been reduced insofar as supply-demand imbalances underlying inflationary pressures persisted. Some imbalances may have worsened. For instance, credit restrictions may have squeezed working capital advanced, particularly for small firms. Thus supply may have been reduced in some cases even more than the contraction in demand. Monetary discipline would then have widened the gap between supply and demand in some sectors to fuel inflation. Even more important, perhaps, was the nature of fiscal adjustment enforced by the stabilization programme. It was bound to push up inflation through higher costs, when subsidies were cut as on fertilizers, administered prices were raised as for petroleum products, or user-charges were hiked by public utilities as for electricity. The tariff reform, which reduced customs duties across-the-board, was sought to be made revenue-neutral (such that total tax revenues remained unaffected) not through an increase in direct taxes that would reduce disposable incomes of the rich and dampen inflation, but through increases in excise duties that would fuel inflation through higher costs which would be passed on to consumers and squeeze real incomes of the poor through higher prices of essential commodities. The substantial depreciation of the rupee, explicit in exchange rate adjustments and implicit in the so-called partial-convertibility or full-convertibility, also contributed to inflation by raising the cost of all imported intermediates and the mark-ups on the domestic sale of many final goods. In the sphere of monetary policy, the high interest rates, which were an integral part of the stabilization programme, probably contributed to cost-push inflation by raising the cost of borrowing finance for firms. However, despite this high interest, liquidity was not tight enough, for the increase in the broad aggregate of money supply, defined as M3, was about 18 per cent per annum throughout the first half of the 1990s which was about the same as the undisciplined monetary expansion of the 1980s. The high interest rates probably attracted foreign capital inflows and contributed to cost-push inflation but did not impose monetary discipline (conforming to monetary targets) as defined by the IMF or the government.

It is almost certain that the rate of inflation would have been even higher were it not for the succession of good monsoons. The reason is simple. The performance of the agricultural sector has always been the crucial determinant of price behaviour in India. Bad harvests fuel inflation and good harvests dampen inflation. Food prices, in particular, lead the general price level and influence inflationary expectations. In this respect, the liberalization programme has been unusually lucky so far. But, in the nature of things, this luck must run out.

We believe that the bounty of the weather gods was neutralized by stabilization policies on the inflation front. The sharp reduction in fertilizer subsidies was made to stand on its head by a peculiar compromise: a more than compensatory increase in the procurement prices of foodgrains. This contributed strongly to inflation. The objective of restraining food subsidies led to a sharp increase in the issue prices of foodgrains in the public distribution system. Consequently, the procurement prices of common paddy and wheat, paid to producers, were raised by more than 50 per cent between 1990-91 and 1993-94. At the same time, issue prices in the public distribution system, charged to consumers, were raised even more, by 86 per cent for common rice and by 72 per cent for wheat, betweeen mid-1990 and early 1994. These increases exercised an important influence on market prices of foodgrains and, in turn, on inflation. Consequently, between end-March 1990 and end-March 1995, prices of foodgrains rose by 90 per cent. The rate of inflation was almost as high for many other necessities. Over the same period, prices of primary food articles (cereals, pulses, fruits, vegetables, eggs, fish, meat and spices) rose by almost 80 per cent, while the prices of manufactured food products (sugar, edible oils and processed foods) rose by more than 60 per cent. The persistence of double-digit inflation was on the whole more pronounced in essential commodities. As a result, the poor were hit the hardest. At the same time, the cumulative impact of a substantial increase in the cost of living index created pressures for raising wages and salaries. The architects of liberalization, who failed to control inflation, could only preach wage restraint. Not surprisingly, few have been persuaded.

Fiscal Crisis

In the IMF world of orthodox economics, the objective of fiscal adjustment is to narrow the gap between income and expenditure of the government. It is meant to reduce domestic borrowing by the government not only from the central bank but also from the people. Naturally, this has also been attempted in India but the outcome can hardly be described as a success. The gross fiscal deficit of the central government has moved like a yo-yo : it was reduced from 8.4 per cent of GDP in 1990-91 (and an average of 8.2 per cent of GDP in the second half of the 1980s) to 5.9 per cent of GDP in 1991-92; it went down to 5.7 per cent of GDP in 1992-93 but rose to 7.7 per cent of GDP in 1993-94 and is estimated at about 7 per cent of GDP in 1994-95. It would seem that the government tightened its belt for two years but lost the battle of the fiscal bulge thereafter.

The problem, however, is with the quality rather than the quantity of adjustment. The fiscal adjustment embodied in the budgets of the central government has relied on a surplus in the capital account (transactions which affect its net wealth or debt position) to finance a deficit in the revenue account (transactions which affect its income or expenditure). This is because the focus of IMF-sponsored adjustment, accepted by our government in a mindless manner, is on the fiscal deficit rather than on the revenue deficit of the government. But the cause for concern lies elsewhere. The revenue deficit of the central government remained at 2.6 per cent of GDP in both 1991-92 and 1992-93. Indeed, it was the same as it was during the second half of the 1980s. It jumped to 4.2 per cent of GDP in 1993-94 and is estimated at 3.8 per cent of GDP in 1994-95. In other words, the government has continued to borrow as much as 2.6 per cent of GDP every year for a long time, and now more than 4 per cent of GDP, to finance its consumption expenditure. Ideally, there should be a revenue surplus large enough to finance capital expenditure on defence and in the social sectors, where there are no immediate or tangible returns. This would permit borrowing only to finance capital account expenditure that yields a steady income flow to the exchequer. So long as that income flow exceeds the burden of servicing accumulated debt, government borrowing remains sustainable. The reality in India, despite fiscal adjustment, is exactly the opposite. Our present fiscal regime, which borrows to support consumption, and cuts investment which could create productive capacities and future income flows, is simply not sustainable over time.

It needs to be said that the size of the deficit or the amount of borrowing are the symptoms and not the disease. The real problem, as we have stressed earlier, is the use to which government expenditure is put in relation to the cost of borrowing by the government. The cost of the borrowing has risen significantly since the onset of economic liberalization for two reasons. First, the government has cut back sharply on its borrowing at low interest rates from the Reserve Bank of India. Second, compared with the past, the government is now borrowing much larger amounts, and at a significantly higher cost, from the commercial banking system and the domestic capital market because interest rates on government securities have been raised to market levels. On the other hand, the use of the borrowing in the era of economic liberalization remains as unproductive as before. If anything, a much higher proportion of government borrowing is now being used to finance consumption expenditure which yields no return. There is no discernible effort to increase the productivity of investment expenditure. Even worse, the level of investment expenditure has declined because the process of fiscal adjustment has created a massive squeeze on public investment. In the Union Budgets from 1991-92 to 1994-95, the period of adjustment, the provision for capital expenditure in the Central Plan and in the Central Plan assistance for the States—perhaps the best aggregate measure of resources allocated to finance public investment—remained at about the same level in nominal terms (and was not discernibly higher than in 1990-91). It is obvious that these budget provisions did not even compensate for inflation, let alone the substantial devaluation of the rupee, so that public investment financed by the central government declined sharply in real terms. This fiscal squeeze meant that the state governments did not fare any better. In fact, they probably fared worse as overdraft facilities for state governments, with the Reserve Bank of India, were strictly enforced. Clearly, such a pattern of adjustment is not even intended to provide a sustainable solution to the fiscal crisis. It only postpones the day of reckoning.

Growth

The short-term impact of IMF-style macro-economic adjustment on output and growth has been almost uniformly adverse across countries in Latin America, Sub-Saharan Africa, East Europe or South Asia. The stabilization experience in India is no exception. In real terms, GDP growth was 1.1 per cent in 1991-92, 4 per cent in 1992-93 and 4.1 per cent in 1993-94. These trends are, in large part, attributable to the performance of the agricultural sector which was poor in 1991-92 (-2.7 per cent), robust in 1992-93 (5.3 per cent) and good in 1993-94 (3 per cent). Thus the monsoon factor controlled by our weather gods rather than the liberalization factor controlled by our Finance Ministry lords was decisive. Leaving aside agriculture, manufacturing output dropped by 2.7 per cent in 1991-92, rose by a meagre 2 per cent in 1992-93 and increased by 3.6 per cent in 1993-94. (National accounts statistics on growth rates in 1994-95 are not yet available). These developments are in sharp contrast with rates of growth during the second half of the 1980s when growth in GDP was 6.4 per cent per annum, growth in agricultural production was 5.3 per cent per annum and growth in manufacturing output was 7.5 per cent per annum.

It is important to understand the economic factors underlying these trends. For any given productivity of investment, the impact of adjustment on growth depends upon what happens to the *level* of investment in real terms and the *rate* of investment as a proportion of GDP.

In the public sector as a whole, which is made up of the central government, the state governments and public enterprises, gross investment at constant 1980-81 prices experienced a stagnation at about Rs 200 billion during the period from 1991-92 to 1993-94 and did not even recover to the level attained in 1990-91. This was obviously attributable to the fiscal adjustment in the stabilization programme which axed public investment ruthlessly. In the private sector, which is made up of the household sector and the corporate sector, the trend was similar as gross domestic investment at constant 1980-81 prices fluctuated in the range of Rs 300-350 billion over the same period, but did not quite return to the level reached in 1990-91. It would seem that the squeeze on public investment induced by fiscal adjustment, combined with monetary discipline, had a dampening effect on private investment. Standard American text books, from which both the economists in the IMF and presumably the mandarins in our Ministry of Finance draw their 'wisdom', propound a theory in which larger public investment 'crowds out' private investment. Conversely, according to this theory, smaller public investment should be compensated by an increase in private investment. This largely ideological view that public and private investment are competitive rather than complementary has found little empirical support in India, either in common experience or in econometric studies. The reason for this is not far to seek. A higher level of government investment raises the demand for all types of goods in the economy several times (through what economists call the 'multiplier mechanism') and this, in turn, raises capacity utilization in the private sector. As a result, both private profitability and private investment tend to rise with government investment. Therefore, without an increase in the level of public investment in real terms, economic growth is most likely to be constrained in India, because even private investment will slacken.

But that is not all. The nature of macro-economic adjustment in India has been such that it is almost certain to have adverse implications for economic growth in the medium term. As a proportion of GDP, gross domestic investment registered a sharp decline during the period of stabilization, mainly because of the said complementarity between public and private investment. Domestic savings, which tend to be governed largely by domestic investment, because investment determines aggregate demand and aggregate income (from which savings come), also fell as a result. So much so that, between 1990-91 and 1993-94, the saving-GDP ratio dropped by almost 4 percentage points (from 23.9 to 20.2 per cent) while the investment-GDP ratio dropped by 7 percentage points (from 27.4 per cent to 20.4 per cent). The decline in net domestic saving and net domestic investment (when depreciation is netted out), as a proportion of net domestic product, was even more pronounced. In the process of macro-economic adjustment, insofar as investment still exceeds domestic saving, a corresponding excess of imports over exports bridges the gap. In other words, the shortfall in domestic savings is being financed by foreign capital inflows which represent foreign savings.

Economic growth can come, in part, from an increase in the productivity of investment. But only in part. Ultimately, sustained economic growth also requires an increase in the rate of investment. And if the rate of investment is so much lower than before, it would require a corresponding increase in the productivity of investment just to maintain the earlier rate of economic growth. This is simple arithmetic. It must also be recognized that the level and the productivity of investment are interdependent variables that tend to move together. Higher investments mean the realization of scale economies, the adoption of latest production techniques and perhaps, most important, infrastructural capital formation whether in education and training or in utilities and overheads. They all raise the productivity of investment directly or indirectly. The misguided policies which have resulted in such a drastic drop in investment in recent years will also dampen productivity growth. Together, they cannot but cripple the prospects of economic growth in the medium-term.

II. ECONOMIC PRIORITIES OF THE PEOPLE

The problems of management of the economy are largely the concern of the government and, with the exception of inflation, do not interest the common people of India. Economic priorities, however, are an altogether different matter. For they must be determined by the needs and the aspirations of the people. Unfortunately, however, these priorities have not received the attention they deserve in democratic India. It is impossible to be exhaustive. But there are issues which are overwhelmingly important simply because they shape the living conditions and the daily existence of the majority of people in our society. Such issues are employment and poverty; agriculture and the rural sector; and infrastructure, both physical and social. Economic liberalization, as it has unfolded so far, does not even address these priorities. Yet, it may directly or indirectly affect these economic priorities. Let us consider the experience since 1991.

Employment and Poverty

We do not, as yet, have data on trends in employment and unemployment during the 1990s. In the absence of direct evidence, it is only possible to put forward a plausible hypothesis about the impact of the stabilization experience and the slowdown in growth on employment. It is reasonable to presume that growth in employment in the agricultural sector was not affected much, insofar as the increase in output was sustained entirely because of the sequence of good monsoons and possibly despite the stabilization policies. In contrast, it is most likely that growth in employment in the industrial sector was dampened by the near-stagnation in output in that sector. This plausible hypothesis is supported by available evidence. The rate of growth of employment in the organized sector of the economy (including both the public sector and the private sector) dropped from more than 1.7 per cent per annum in the late 1980s to 1.2 per cent in 1991-92 and 0.6 per cent in 1992-93. The contraction in public expenditure and the consequent reduction in aggregate demand could not but adversely effect employment in the unorganized sector, whether non-agricultural rural employment or urban informal sector employment, given the casual (non-permanent) nature of such employment. In this context, it is important to remind ourselves that the growth of the labour force in India since independence has always been higher than the growth in employment, so that the backlog of unemployment has grown steadily over time. What is more, employment growth has not even kept pace with output growth. Economists measure this relationship in terms of employment elasticities (proportionate increase in employment divided by the proportionate increase in output). Evidence available suggests that the already low employment elasticities registered a significant decline between the early 1970s and the late 1980s, for the economy as a whole as also for all the major sectors (agriculture, industry and services). Under the circumstances, it is almost certain that both underemployment and open unemployment increased at a more rapid pace in the early 1990s, as growth in output slowed down. It is also plausible to argue that landless labourers in the rural sector and casual wage labour in the urban sector were probably the most adversely affected by the pressure of increasing underemployment and unemployment.

The probable increase in unemployment among the vulnerable sections of the population, during the period of stabilization, coincided with a definite increase in food prices. Research in India has established that rising food prices erode most the real income of these vulnerable sections, pushing them below the minimum nutrition level for human beings which is described, in polite language, as the 'poverty line'. It is, therefore, not surprising that the increase in food prices led to an increase in the incidence of absolute poverty.

The data base for poverty estimates is provided by National Sample Survey tables on consumer expenditure, but these are now compiled only on a quinquennial basis. The results of the round conducted in 1987-88 are published but the results of the round conducted in 1993-94 are not yet available. The National Sample Survey does, however, collect data on consumer expenditure, by decile groups, on an annual basis. But this is based on thin samples, which are not comparable with the complete rounds in terms of either coverage or reliability. All the same, even such limited information is better than mere inference or assertion.

The evidence available shows that, between 1989-90 and 1992-93, the proportion of the population living below the poverty line (defined as a nutritional minimum in terms of calories per day) increased from 34 per cent to 41 per cent, while the number of persons living below the poverty line rose from 282 million to 355 million. The increase was far more pronounced in rural India than it was in urban India. This trend provides a sharp contrast with the steady reduction in the percentage of the population below the poverty line over the entire period from 1972-73 to 1987-88.

There can be little doubt that the major factor underlying this increase in the incidence of poverty was the rapid increase in food prices. The persistence of double-digit inflation in prices of foodgrains, despite the succession of good monsoons, was the immediate reason. It was induced by substantial increases in procurement prices for producers and a more than commensurate increase in the public distribution system prices for consumers. What is more, over this period, there was no discernible increase in the allocation for the public distribution system, while the sales through the public distribution system declined steadily as the difference between ration-shop prices and market prices narrowed to a small margin. Ironically enough, there was a steady accumulation in the stock of foodgrains at the same time. It would seem that the higher procurement prices for producers enabled the government to add to its stockpile of food, some of which would be eaten by rats in warehouses. But the higher issue prices for consumers, dictated by budgetary discipline, meant that these inventories could not be utilized in any way for human consumption. Thus, the public distribution system failed to serve its intended purpose. Strange though it may seem, the budget provisions for subsidies on food may have ended up supporting the costs of carrying stocks more than providing cheap food. The price of food, not only in the market place but also in the ration shops, was simply too high for the poor.

But that is not all. As we have seen, the inflation was nearly as high in other primary food articles and processed food products. Given such inflation in food, and in the prices of essential commodities across the board, it would not be surprising if the incidence of poverty registered a further increase in 1993-94 and 1994-95. In this context, it is worth noting that the purchasing power of the people, even as an arithmetic average, did not register any increase. Indeed, between 1990-91 and 1993-94, both per capita national income (in the range of Rs 2,200 per annum at 1980-81 prices) and per capita final consumer expenditure in the domestic market (in the range of Rs 1,850 per annum at 1980-81 prices) experienced a stagnation or decline in real terms. We would infer that inflation, which was concentrated in the prices of necessities, probably redistributed incomes away from the poor, leaving them worse off. It must have spread poverty in the process.

In a situation where inflation could not be restrained, the government should have endeavoured to protect the consumption levels of the poor by increasing public expenditure destined for them. Strikingly enough, budget support for poverty alleviation programmes declined even in nominal terms and as a proportion of total central government expenditure in 1991-92. That was, perhaps, the first flush of enthusiasm for liberalization. Subsequently, it recovered somewhat in 1992-93 and rose in 1993-94 as a proportion of total central government expenditure. But, at constant prices or as a proportion of GDP, expenditure on anti-poverty programmes in both 1991-92 and 1992-93 was lower than it was in 1989-90 and 1990-91 and was not discernibly higher in 1993-94. Evidence available on performance indicators in terms of quantitative achievements in the two major poverty alleviation programmes for rural India provides further confirmation. The number of families assisted under the Integrated Rural Development Programme, which seeks to promote self-employment among the rural poor by providing productive assets or inputs through a mix of subsidies and bank credit, declined steadily from 3.4 million in 1989-90 to 2 million in 1992-93 and, despite some recovery, remained at 2.5 million in 1993-94. The employment generated under the Jawahar Rozgar Yojana, which seeks to create employment for the rural poor on works that are meant to create productive assets in the rural sector, also declined from 864 million man-days in 1989-90 to 778 million man-days in 1992-93, but rose subsequently to 1,024 million man-days in 1993-94. It should be noted that, in both programmes, the decline was more pronounced in the early years of liberalization, 1991-92 and 1992-93, followed by some restoration in 1993-94. The important fact, however, is that the real value of resources (measured by economists at constant prices) made available for poverty alleviation programmes actually diminished for some time, and did not register the necessary increase thereafter. This was one of the consequences of the misdirected fiscal adjustment by the government. The economic architects of liberalization in India were both insensitive to the poor and dogmatic in their approach; in a period of stabilization and adjustment, more real resources should have been provided to support the poor who are particularly vulnerable in such periods.

It is important to recognize that such programmes for alleviating poverty are essential and may need to be strengthened during the period of difficult economic transition, but cannot provide a permanent solution. Ultimately, the process of economic growth must create employment and incomes for the poor. There is no alternative to this. No other sustainable means of eradicating poverty exists. Consequently, rapid expansion of employment must receive a high priority in any strategy of poverty alleviation.

The Indian development experience thus far has been thoroughly unsatisfactory. Most people who don't find useful and gainful employment have to remain in the countryside in desperate poverty. Post-independence industrial growth failed to provide them with any escape from their poverty by creating adequate employment opportunities in industry or modern services. Indeed, industrial growth was not even enough to absorb the backlog of the unemployed in the cities, let alone surplus labour from the countryside. Moreover, a large part of such employment has been created in low-productivity, low-income occupations in the urban informal sector, mostly in services rather than in manufacturing. The high economic cost of infrastructural investment in the megacities, combined with the rapidly increasing social cost of· negative environmental consequences, require us to reconsider employment expansion in rural India. At first sight, this does not hold out as much promise as one might expect, particularly in the agricultural sector. For one, agriculture already provides almost two-thirds of total employment in the economy although its contribution to GDP is less than one-third. For another, available research suggests that, beyond a certain level of development, employment creation per unit of output growth in agriculture declines. There are, of course, parts of India where agriculture is still extremely backward and agricultural growth would make a significant contribution to employment growth for some time to come but only in these areas. However, the prospect is, in fact, better than it seems at first sight. The constraint on employment creation in agriculture can be relaxed significantly through investment in agriculture.

The potential for expanding the area under cultivation has been largely exhausted almost everywhere in India. The possibilities of increasing yields per hectare through technologies based on seeds and fertilizers have been used up significantly in many parts of the country. Therefore, increased cropping intensity in agriculture mostly through control of water must receive the highest priority. This has a high capacity to absorb labour in agriculture by increasing days of gainful employment roughly from less than 180 days per year to nearly 300 days per year. And its most favourable impact would be on the poorest : agricultural labourers, tenants (or sharecroppers) and marginal farmers. A fundamental precondition for this is extensive control of water, especially through medium and minor irrigation. Elaborate econometric studies show that the shifting of resources from subsidies on fertilizers to investment in irrigation would yield great benefits in terms of agricultural employment, output and growth. This would also spread the benefits by stimulating the expansion of non-agricultural rural employment through supply-demand linkages. The argument developed here also illustrates our general point that government expenditure should be productive. We should be concerned not so much with its reduction as with its better use. The problem with liberalization in India is that it has chosen the soft option of cutting fertilizer subsidies only to increase procurement prices, instead of confronting the genuine choice of increasing irrigation investment at the cost of fertilizer subsidies. In doing so, the architects of economic liberalization seem to be working only for their immediate political survival, but not for broader objectives.

The process of economic liberalization would directly affect employment growth in the industrial sector and in urban India. This impact would be positive if it leads to export expansion in labour-intensive manufacturing activities where India has a potential comparative advantage. This impact could be negative if import liberalization switches domestic demand away from home-produced goods to foreign goods, irrespective of whether it enforces efficiency or closures at a micro-level, for it would have an adverse effect on output (hence employment) at the macro-level which would be magnified through what economists call the multiplier effect. Such a magnified contraction is most likely in the sphere of consumer goods, where import liberalization is on the cards. The consumer goods sector contributes about one-third of output and provides roughly two-thirds of employment in the manufacturing sector : much of it in the small-scale sector which is that much more vulnerable. The vulnerability to import liberalization would not be confined only to the reduction in employment due to direct substitution in favour of imported goods.

This contraction in employment would multiply through the consequent decline in purchasing power, reducing output and employment elsewhere in the economy through successive rounds of the same multiplier mechanism.

There is another dimension to the problem of employment in the industrial sector which is worth noting. In so far as economic liberalization increases the average productivity of labour, through the use of capital intensive or labour saving foreign technology or through a restructuring of firms which increases efficiency, it will reduce the contribution of any given rate of economic growth to employment growth. The only way out is to increase the rate of economic growth in proportion to labour productivity growth. But this has not happened so far under India's liberalization programme.

To sum up, employment growth requires labour absorption both inside and outside agriculture. The present pattern of economic liberalization in India is guilty of of commission as well as errors of omission. Its error of omission is agriculture, where little attention has been paid, especially to irrigation. Its error of commission is in industry where employment growth will be dampened because of cuts in public investment, unthinking import liberalization and non-selective use of foreign technology.

Agriculture and the Rural Sector

The entire debate about economic liberalization proceeds as if the agricultural sector or rural India does not exist or, if it exists, it does not matter. This is incredible in an economy where two-thirds of the work force is employed in agriculture and where three-fourths of the population lives in the rural sector. Even if their share of income in the economy is much smaller than their proportion in the population, it must be remembered that their share of votes in the polity is directly proportional. The electoral, if not political, compulsions of a democracy cannot be set aside for long.

No sensible restructuring of the Indian economy is even thinkable without a clear perspective on agriculture. And it is not as if the agricultural sector is without structural rigidities or structural imbalances. The process of economic liberalization will, therefore, be constrained by what happens in the agricultural sector. Obversely, this process is also bound to have a significant impact on Indian agriculture. It has reduced fertilizer subsidies and priority sector lending, and it has moved domestic prices of inputs and outputs closer to world prices. These measures will have widespread repercussions.

The increase in fertilizer prices and the increase in the price (or decrease in the volume) of credit are particularly problematic. This is because, given the stagnation and decline of public investment in the agricultural sector which began in the late 1970s prior to liberalization, the use of fertilizers and the availability of credit have become the most important determinants of the increase in yields per hectare and, hence, of agricultural output. The attempt to reduce fertilizer subsidies during the period of liberalization *without* any increase in investment in irrigation has made matters worse for agriculture. Available evidence shows the consequence of following a combination of wrong policies. The period from 1990-91 to 1993-94 witnessed a stagnation in the total consumption of fertilizers in the economy. In real terms, gross investment in the agricultural sector also experienced a stagnation over this period. The uneven increase in prices of fertilizers caused by retaining a part of the subsidy on nitrogenous fertilizers but removing it altogether on phosphatic and potassic fertilizers has created imbalances in fertilizer useage as the consumption of phosphatic and potassic fertilizers declined in absolute terms. Fiscal adjustment has meant a continued or even sharper decline of public investment, at constant prices, in the agricultural sector. These developments during the first half of the 1990s mean accumulating problems for the agricultural sector which will surface when the weather gods cease to be kind.

Economic liberalization has also meant trade policy reform affecting agriculture. Its main objectives are twofold. It seeks to dismantle restrictions on trade other than tariffs and wishes to bring domestic prices closer to world prices. This represents a radical departure from the past, particularly in the sphere of agriculture where foreign trade was used as a residual to bridge the difference between domestic production and domestic consumption. Domestic prices of agricultural commodities in India were much lower, and more stable than world prices. This is as it should have been, given that the average income level in India is only a small fraction of what it is in the world outside. Any attempt to equalize domestic prices with world prices may set in motion forces strong enough to reshape the whole process of economic reform. The impact of agricultural price liberalization will not be confined to trade flows. It will extend to output and prices. The latter will make the economy more prone to inflation. The changes in the distribution of agricultural output and incomes between regions may accentuate inequalities, which would have political implications. The increase in domestic prices of essential commodities produced in the agricultural sector is bound to erode food security, and heighten concerns about the cost of living, which in turn will have social repurcussions. There may not be much comfort in the balance of payments either. This is partly because India's share in world output for many agricultural commodities is high, and partly because a relatively small proportion of world output enters into world trade. Thus, how much India buys or sells in world markets would affect world prices significantly. An increase in the volume of India's agricultural imports or exports is likely to raise the prices paid for imports or lower the prices received for exports by India in the world market. At the same time, many structural rigidities in the agricultural sector inhibit large supply responses by farmers to price incentives at least in the short run. These difficulties do not mean that the trade policy regime for agriculture did not need simplification. It did. Consideration of comparative advantage should also become an integral part of domestic economic policies vis-a-vis agriculture, both while drawing up plans for infrastructural investment and while setting procurement or support prices. However, all this requires more, and not less, careful intervention by the government which seems to go against the current mood to liberalize. We should not forget the crucial role of the government, especially in the early phase of the 'green revolution'. The role of the government will be just as important in shifting from subsidies on fertilizers to investment in irrigation. The government must not treat economic liberalization as an excuse for abandoning its strategic role in agricultural development. Any such abdication of responsibility only means that we miss out on the genuine economic priorities of the country in chasing a mirage of the market.

It has been said that India lives in its villages. The advocates of economic liberalization are not concerned, for their object is to integrate with the affluence of the world outside and not think about the poverty of rural India. But even the representatives of the people who rule India, it would seem, do not care except, perhaps, around election time. Four decades of planned economic development did little to narrow the gap between the villages and the cities of India. Rural-urban disparities remained vast. It is instructive to consider some evidence, for the year 1991, on this rural-urban divide. In rural India, GDP per capita was only one-third what it was in urban India. The literacy rates were 58 per cent for males and 30 per cent for females in rural India as compared with 81 per cent for males and 64 per cent for females in urban India. Infant mortality rates were as high as 82 per 1000 in rural India as compared with 45 per 1000 in urban India. Rural India, which is home for 75 per cent of our population, had only 31 per cent of the hospitals, 48 per cent of the dispensaries, 27 per cent of the medical personnel (doctors, nurses and health workers) and only 18 per cent of the beds for patients. More than 25 per cent of the population in rural India did not have access to drinking water supply while this proportion was lower at 15 per cent of the urban population. As much as 97 per cent of the rural population did not have access to sanitation facilities, while this proportion was much lower at 54 per cent of the urban population. Such evidence could be piled up. It would only confirm the massive rural-urban differences in the quality of life. Yet, it is seldom recognized that the living conditions of even the rich peasants in rural India are much worse than the living conditions of white-collar or blue-collar workers in urban India. The irony is that many on the left of the political spectrum think of the former (with some hostility) as the 'rural elite' and the latter (with some empathy) as the 'working class'.

Economic reforms in India are likely to widen rather than narrow the rural-urban divide, for the process of economic liberalization has an unmistakable urban bias. The problem, however, is not simply the neglect of rural India on the liberalization agenda. It is more complex. Economic liberalization means that production and investment decisions will be based on market forces. And markets allocate resources, in the pursuit of profit, in accordance with purchasing power rather than need. There may, then, be a cumulative causation which creates more and more income in urban areas but less and less in rural areas. It is important to remember that any further widening of rural-urban disparities in the economy is bound to worsen problems in polity and society. India may then die rather than live in its villages. And the market-worship of liberalization will have to take its share of the blame.

Infrastructure

For the common man in India, mere existence is difficult and living is no easy matter. What can be taken for granted by people in most societies is a desperate struggle here. The infrastructure which exists simply cannot provide the population with facilities that would be a bare minimum elsewhere. The roads are full of potholes. Rural roads are even worse, for they are submerged or washed away in the monsoons. Public transport on the roads is unreliable, unsafe and inadequate. There is not enough room in the trains and reservations must be made months in advance. The supply of electricity is uncertain and erratic. The telephones work in a whimsical manner. The postal system, once the pride of India, has slowed down and one can no longer be sure that letters will be delivered. Drinking water, which is available for a few hours in the day, is not safe as infections abound. For a substantial proportion of the population, sanitation facilities do not exist. Housing is poor: large numbers of people do not have a roof over their heads, while many have to pay exorbitant rents they can barely afford. The number of schools is not enough and the quality of education is poor. Medical services are scarce. Public health care and hygiene systems are almost non-existent. Environmental conditions deteriorate by the day. The hapless citizen often comes to the conclusion that nothing works and nobody cares. It is only money or influence that can provide an escape from this reality.

It is apparent that the physical infrastructure is straining at the seams. This makes life difficult for all. But it also introduces bottlenecks that constrain production and distribution in the economy. It is obvious that the social infrastructure is woefully inadequate. This worsens the living conditions of the people, particularly the poor who find it difficult to meet their minimum needs. The process of economic liberalization does not offer an improved prospect. It could end up making matters worse.

Consider, first, the physical infrastructure. The basic philosophy underlying economic liberalization is that the public sector is inefficient and that the State must withdraw to create space for the private sector. The compulsions of fiscal adjustment have only reinforced this mode of thinking. The resource crunch has been particularly acute for public investment in infrastructure. The budget support provided by the central government for the key infrastructure sectors—energy, transport and communications—has registered a significant decline during the period 1989-90 to 1993-94, not only as a proportion of total central government expenditure (from 8.5 per cent to 4.5 per cent) but also as a proportion of GDP (from 1.75 per cent to 0.81 per cent). In real terms, such investment expenditure has contracted by nearly 50 per cent over the period (from Rs 39 billion to Rs 21 billion at 1980-81 prices). This has not posed any political problem because there are no constiteuencies for such investment expenditure and no interest group complains or protests. The fiscal squeeze has also reduced the degrees of freedom for state governments and they have cut back on public investment in infrastructure. For them, as for the central government, it is easier to reduce such investment expenditure than to squeeze consumption expenditure. These cuts are bound to constrain the supply response of the economy in the medium-term. For it is the physical infrastructure which determines an economy's absorptive capacity for investment. It is hoped that private investment, both domestic and foreign, will be a substitute for public investment in infrastructure. These hopes have been belied so far because private investment in infrastructural sectors is constrained by the large critical minimum scale, the long gestation lags and the high risks. This should come as no surprise because the financing of private investment in infrastructure has posed problems everywhere in the developing world. Even in Mrs Thatcher's Britain, attempts to privatize infrastructure often meant additional problems, not solutions. This lesson should be learnt now. No government, whether on the right or on the left, can shun its responsibility in the creation and maintenance of infrastructure. Foreign investors cannot and will not do the job that central, state or local governments are supposed to do. And where they do come, as Enron in the power sector, the price may amount to a pound of flesh.

Consider, next, the social infrastructure. Indicators of social development suggest that India has made progress in the four decades from 1951 to 1991. Life expectancy at birth has doubled, infant mortality rates have halved and the literacy rate has trebled. There is evidence that health care, housing and education are better. The proportion of the population that has access to electricity, drinking water and sanitation facilities is notably higher. Yet much remains to be done. Almost half the population is still illiterate. Infant mortality rates are still inordinately high. Enrolment ratios at primary school are very low. And, as suggested above, the social infrastructure is poor in absolute terms when we consider basic human needs. What is more, India fares poorly in international comparisons of social development among developing countries. But we must remember that much of this discussion is based on arithmetic averages. In fact, the availability of or access to social infrastructure is uneven between social groups, economic classes and geographical regions. Segments of the population, say scheduled castes or scheduled tribes in particular and the poor in general, may experience what is now described as social exclusion.

There was a significant increase in the resources provided by the government for expenditure on social sectors during the 1980s. Unfortunately, this has not continued since liberalization began. The attempt at stabilization and adjustment by the government was the underlying reason. During the period from 1989-90 to 1993-94, the budgetary allocations for the social sectors by the central government stagnated in real terms and remained unchanged as a proportion of GDP. The trend in the budgetary provisions made by the state governments for the social sectors was about the same. Consequently, for the centre and the states, taken together, the expenditure on social sectors stagnated in the range of 6 per cent of GDP. And there are no immediate political constiteuncies that would have claimed or demanded more resources for social consumption. The increases envisaged in the Eighth Plan, which were essential during this period of adjustment, simply did not materialize. The medium-term impact of economic liberalization has, therefore, been negative. The long-term impact cannot be beneficial either because private investment in social infrastructure has been, and will remain, confined to services for the affluent sections of the population. Specialized nursing homes, luxury housing estates, expensive private schools, privatized higher education and so on may win vocal supporters for liberalization but they do not represent India's needs or priorities. The poor who need these services cannot create a demand in the market because they do not have the purchasing power. Liberalization, it seems, has tied both their hands : by curbing employment opportunities, and by neglecting the provision of social services. It should be abundantly clear that the social infrastructure for the majority of our people would have to be financed by the government and the services rendered would have to be provided through institutions managed by the government. Thus, pressures must be mounted in every way to improve the performance of the government and to ensure that it does not abdicate its responsibilities in the name of liberalization.

III. DEVELOPMENT OBJECTIVES IN THE LONG RUN

We pointed out earlier that any process of economic liberalization which is crisis driven, or guided by IMF programmes of stabilization and World Bank programmes of structural adjustment, is likely to neglect long-term development objectives. This happens for two reasons. For one, such objectives cannot be defined in terms of mechanical performance criteria laid down by the multilateral financial institutions. For another, such objectives do not bring tangible gains in politics which can be exploited by governments in one term to seek a majority verdict. Our democracy is no exception. The way out of this dilemma is to get our own priorities right. And development objectives which are important in the long run should receive the much deserved attention. There are three, in particular, that are pressing : education and human resource development; acquisition of technological capabilities; and managing regional disparities in a federal context. Such issues may appear unimportant in the context of the present technocratic mumbo-jumbo of fiscal correction, but must be addressed by any leadership which can think ahead. This needs a vision about the future of economy, polity and society, not for the next month, the next year or the next election but for the next 25 years. There was such a vision, however imperfect, at the time of independence, which we have now lost.

Human Resources

In a long term perspective, the neglect of education and human resource development is among the most important failures to emerge from the Indian experience of economic development in the post-colonial era. Strangely enough, the liberalization agenda simply does not address this failure. It is worth noting that there is no mention of education, let alone human resource development, in the reform process. And yet, any attempt to globalize requires that our levels of education and skill formation are brought to a level where we can be internationally competitive. We often lull ourselves into the false comfort that India has some highly trained persons. But we must recognize that one drop of rain does not make a monsoon. Nor does a handful of highly qualified people make a vast population internationally competitive in terms of skills and training. Without recognizing these implications, stabilization and adjustment has meant some contraction in the real value of resources allocated by the government to education. Unless we invest enough in human beings, which will require substantial increases in resources provided for education, productivity increases may not follow structural reform. And in the absence of sufficiently developed human resources the benefits of integrating with the world economy will simply elude us. Yet, even those who are high on the rhetoric of becoming global players do not seem to understand this simple proposition.

In this context, we would like to emphasize that the spread of education in society was, in a sense, crucial for the economic development of late industrializers, particularly the success stories of East Asia that are now perceived as role models. It would seem that the architects of economic liberalization in India do not recognize the significance of these lessons which emerge from experience elsewhere. Human resource development is both means and an end. It is a means of raising levels of productivity and mobilizing our most abundant resource (labour) for the purpose of development. It is an end in so far as it makes a basic contribution to an improvement in the quality of life, for people as individuals and for society at large. Education, then, is not simply a part of the social infrastructure. It is a priority, not only for the present but also for the future. The relative importance of its components may change over time : from primary education and adult literacy through vocational education to higher education, technical education or professional education. But investing in human beings is always important, at every stage of development. The returns to society may accrue after a time lag but are always high. Some examples would help. Family planning and population control which are an essential aspect of India's development will gain in momentum with the spread of education, especially among women. Similarly, basic community health and preventive medicine programmes can catch on much faster only in a society where education is spreading rapidly. Productivity increase in manufacturing activities requires labour training and vocational skills which must be provided through education. The importance of basic education is even greater in the context of the ongoing technological revolution which is driven by information technology. We could multiply these examples. The essential point is that returns from investment in education accrue to society in many ways. There is, also, nothing wrong in allowing private initiative and investment in this pursuit, so long as it complements rather than substitutes public responsibility.

Technological Capabilities

The industrialization experience of India suggests that we created a broad base in the 1950s and 1960s but then lost the cutting edge. There are many sectors of the economy where the level of technological development is just not adequate by international standards. There are far too many distressing examples of situations where technologies were imported for particular sectors at a point in time but the import of such technologies has been followed by stagnation rather than adaptation, diffusion and innovation at home. At the same time, in many cases, indigenous development of technology has not led to widespread diffusion, let alone technological upgradation. Although the underlying reasons are complex, it is clear that market structures and government policies have not combined to provide an environment that would encourage the absorption of imported technology and speed up the development of indigenous technology, or create a milieu that would be conducive to diffusion and innovation. It is seldom mentioned that the record of the private sector has been dismal in this sphere. Indeed, the R&D effort in the private corporate sector has been minimal. There is a curious asymmetry in the lessons that economic liberalizers have drawn, or not drawn, from this experience.

The lesson that has been learnt is that there must be a liberal access to imports of technology and it is an important lesson. But an industrializing economy must be able to make a transition from importation to diffusion and innovation, at least in some sectors so that the acquisition of technology through imports is, after a time, followed by the development of domestic technological capabilities. An open regime for the import of technology cannot suffice, for the discipline of the market cannot restrain the recurrence of such imports by domestic firms time after time. Such firms are much like the school boy who can find some one else to write the examinations for him year after year and thus never learns. Domestic technological capabilities may not emerge either because there is no incentive to learn (imports are possible) or because they are stifled (imports are better). The problem may be accentuated in sectors where technical progress is rapid and obsolescence is high.

The lesson that has not been learnt is that the role of the government is crucial for planning technological development across sectors and over time. The instinctive dislike of our liberalizers for big government must be set aside here. This means planning for selective acquisition of technology where it is to be imported, setting aside resources for technology where it is to be produced at home, or even deciding to opt out of a technology where it is not needed. For this purpose, it is necessary to formulate a policy regime for the import of technology, allocate resources for R&D and evolve government procurement policies. In the absence of such strategic intervention by the government, Japan would never have produced automobiles or optical instruments that could compete with their European or American counterparts, Europe would never have produced the airbus that could compete with

Boeing aircraft, and Korea would never have produced consumer electronics that would compete with established Japanese brand names. Let it also be remembered here that, despite heavy initial investment, Japan decided to pull out of aircraft production when things did not come up to the mark. Industrial policy must mean both carrot and stick : reward for international success through unstinted government support but punishment for failure through withdrawal of government support. For industrial policy in a developing country of India's vast size, it is not the market alone but also the government that must be active in this game of reward and punishment.

It is one of the unambiguous lessons of recent economic history that the guiding and supportive role of the State, at a macro-level, is a necessary condition for the development of competitive technological capability in countries that are latecomers to industrialization. And there is no country that has succeeded at industrialization without developing such technological capabilities in firms at a micro-level. In the long-term, the development of technological capabilities is the essential foundation on which international competitiveness is built.

Regional Disparities and Federalism

The process of economic growth is characterized by uneven development across geographical space which tends to increase regional disparities over time. This happens not only in large continental economies but even in smaller economies. In a country of India's size and diversity, however, it raises problems in polity and society which often surface in the form of the religious, language or caste identities. These problems are not new but are pressing, and can get out of hand through manipulation by dishonest politicians. One must be alert to this danger. And it is important to recognize that economic liberalization tends to widen regional disparities because there is a cumulative causation which creates market-driven virtuous circles or vicious circles. Regions that are better endowed with natural resources, physical infrastructure, educated (or skilled) labour and so on, experience a rapid growth. Like magnets, they attract resources and people from elsewhere and the attraction may extend even beyond national boundaries. Contrariwise, disadvantaged regions tend to lag behind and become even more disadvantaged. Indeed, many of them experience an outflow of capital and labour. Over time, the gap widens through such cumulative causation. We have seen this happen, most recently, in Asia. The economic disparities between coastal China in the East and the hinterland in the West are much greater than before. In Indonesia, the economic gap between Java and the other islands is much wider. In Thailand, there is increasing prosperity around Bangkok but poverty persists in the hinterland. In India, some regions already have a distinct economic lead that may become more pronounced with liberalization.

These are real problems that aggravate tensions in economy and society, irrespective of the political system. Examples abound: the erstwhile USSR, what was once Yugoslavia, or even Canada. In a country such as India, where regional disparities co-exist with economic and social divides, we must be conscious of the long term consequences of economic liberalization. Economic disparities between regions are bound to grow. If globalization turns into a secession of the successful, it could have an analogue in terms of a secession of the deprived and we could end up with more separatist movements. These problems need resolution before they blow up.

The political framework of our democracy is both a challenge and an opportunity. It is a challenge because change is far more difficult to manage. It is an opportunity because it provides room for evolving stable coalitions. However, coalitions are stable so long as each partner sees the advantage in federalism. And, in our democratic system, devolution—from the centre to the states and from the states to the districts—is essential to strengthen federalism in a genuine sense. Because only devolution gives real power to the smaller units to decide voluntarily on the extent of cooperation.It is only when they decide to cooperate voluntarily that federalism (and not centralism) succeeds, with democracy meeting the challenge and exploiting the opportunity. But this requires an open and transparent government policy, often contrary to the market, to invest much more in the (physical and social) infrastructure of backward regions. On the other hand, more advanced regions can play by the market. It is in this sense that government intervention and market initiative can complement each other to strengthen, and not to weaken, the prospects of voluntary coalitions and federalism in India. It goes without saying that such management of change needs a long-term vision of economy, polity and society.

Chapter 5

The State and the Market : The Name of the Game

Chapter 5

The State and the Market : The Name of the
Game

The second half of the twentieth century has witnessed a complete swing of the pendulum in the popular mood, as thinking about the role of the State in economic development has undergone a dramatic change. We appear to have moved from a widespread belief, prevalent in the 1950s, that the State could do nothing wrong to a gathering conviction, fashionable in the 1990s, that the State can get nothing right. These are caricatures of perceptions, but the disillusionment with the role of the State, it seems, is shared by economists, politicians and opinion-makers alike. The reality, however, is more complex. Simplified ideas reduced to catchy slogans are somewhat like fads that may be in or out of fashion. They hardly capture the real issues.

The dramatic change in thinking can be attributed in part to ideology and in part to reality. The world of competing ideologies, capitalism versus communism, has given way to a world with a single dominant political ideology. Communism has collapsed and capitalism has emerged triumphant. For some, this happening is so momentous that it has been described as the 'end of history'! The reality that we observe around us has also made its contribution. The market economies of East Asia epitomize success. The erstwhile planned economies of East Europe, in particular the former Soviet Union, represent failure. The success of the market shines when juxtaposed with the failure of the State. However, this is an oversimplified perception. For market failure is also a fact of life. And markets fail badly. The high levels of unemployment in Western Europe, where capitalism began life, are a case in point. But the enthusiasm for economic liberalization is such that it reinforces this asymmetrical view of the State and the market. Indeed, the oversimplified rhetoric of liberalization paints the State as black and the market as white. It leaves no room for grey areas.

Such oversimplification may be convenient for ideology. It does not help clear thinking. Inconvenient questions must be asked even if they do not conform to the fashion of the time. Is it appropriate to pose the problem simply as a choice between government failure and market failure? Ideologues, both on the right and on the left, are inclined to do so. However, this is wrong because it creates a false debate which leads nowhere. Is it necessary to redefine the economic role of the State, particularly in India? In our view, such rethinking is essential. Our basic hypothesis is simple. The State and the market are, in general, complements rather than substitutes. Cooperation rather than conflict should define the relationship between these two institutions. What is more, the relationship between the State and the market cannot be defined once and for all but must change over time in an adaptive manner. Is this feasible in terms of politics, given the nature of the State in India? We think so. This chapter explores these questions and explains the basis of our thinking.

I. GOVERNMENT FAILURE AND MARKET FAILURE

The term 'market failure' has been in the jargon of economists for quite some time. The term 'government failure' has entered their lexicon relatively recently, although Adam Smith was aware of it two centuries ago. It is obvious that the word failure is used to describe outcomes that are inefficient or undesirable with reference to some idealized state of economy and society. For the concerned citizen, however, it is important to understand in simple terms how State intervention fails or why markets fail. Such an understanding is crucial to follow the debate on economic liberalization, particularly if one does not wish to be mystified or fooled by the jargon of economists.

Government failure takes many forms and is attributable to many factors. Most charitably, governments make mistakes because they do not have adequate information about a problem. Quite often, governments do not quite understand the nature of the problem. Without adequate information and necessary understanding, governments are neither able to predict nor able to control the consequences of their actions. Hence, government intervention may not resolve the problem it intends to. Instead, it may lead to unwanted adverse effects that are unintended. There is, often, a divergence between the conception and the design of intervention by the government. The divergence between the design and the implementation of policies is, perhaps, even greater. In fact, between the intention and the reality falls the shadow of bureaucratic arbitrariness.

All this may be true even with the best of intentions on the part of a government. But governments do not always act in the interests of the people at large. Indeed, governments are frequently sectarian in their actions and interventions as they seek to promote or to protect the interests of classes, or groups, whom they represent. More narrowly, they manipulate on behalf of groups who can exercise influence. These reasons lead conservative economics to the conclusion that intervention in markets is inefficient because governments are incapable of intervening efficiently. For those who are so convinced about the inevitability of government failure, the existence of market failure no longer provides an acceptable basis for intervention.

The people, however, are not concerned with abstractions.

127

Their perceptions about government failures are based on observation and experience in the concrete. They observe that governments are usually bad managers of state enterprises in the public sector. More often than not, even the management of the economy by the government leaves much to be desired, especially if rates of inflation or levels of unemployment are unacceptably high. The apparatus of the government is often used deliberately to promote the interests of the ruling elite. This does not surprise anyone. But the governmental system is also used to further, crudely and openly, the interests of powerful individuals through corruption and nepotism. In extreme situations, the State is used as private property or even family property. The disillusionment of the people with the State is understandable.

The most important source of popular disillusionment, of course, is the interface of the citizen with the State. The brush of the ordinary people with the apparatus of government invariably produces something unpleasant to remember. Everybody in India will be able to recall innumerable instances of harassment : anyone who has attempted to obtain an electricity connection or settle a disputed electricity bill; anyone who has been to the office of a municipal corporation (no matter which political party runs it) whether to get a birth or a death certificate or to seek permission to build a modest house; anyone who has dealt with income tax authorities who often specialise in harassing the honest tax payer while tax evaders prosper; anyone in a small business who has had to cope with an excise inspector or a factory inspector; anyone who has applied for a passport or simply wanted to enquire about it at the passport office; anyone who has attempted to lodge a report or a complaint at a police station; anyone who has needed a document from a *patwari* or a *tehsildar*; any small farmer who has sought to obtain seeds and fertilizers from the block development office, or irrigation water from the local functionary of the canals department or power at a concessional tariff from the electircity board outlet;

and so on. The reaction of the helpless citizen ranges from frustration through anger to despair. Liberalization capitalizes on the disillusionment that comes from such daily experiences. But it must be ' recognized that many of these functions (say birth certificates, passports or tax collection) are exclusively in the domain of government everywhere and will remain so. The task here is to improve the performance of the government, for in such activities it cannot be replaced by private enterprise. Thus, even in principle, economic liberalization can address only that subset of government failures which arise because the government intervenes wrongly or attempts to perform the function of the market.

In passing, it is worth noting that such experiences are not unique to India. This has happened elsewhere. In many countries, particularly in the erstwhile socialist countries, the State has attempted to do too much of what it cannot or should not do, while it has done too little of what it can or should do. Some countries in the developing world have been through similar experiences. This is responsible for the disillusionment of citizens with governments. Free market ideology gathered momentum as ordinary people sank into despair under aribitrary bureaucratic controls in these countries. The other side of the hedge, namely the market system, looked much greener, until these government failures began to be overshadowed by market failures. (The 'reformed communists' were voted back to power and over-zealous 'market reformers' lost elections almost everywhere in the erstwhile socialist countries of East Europe including the former Soviet Union.)

It is not altogether surprising that most people are familiar with failures of governments through their experiences. However, most people are much less conscious of failures of markets because these failures look impersonal and natural. They are difficult to recognize. To many conservative economists, market failures appear natural events, somewhat like acts of God, say an earthquake or a flood. But the reasons underlying market failure should not be confined to the domain of economics, nor should market failure be treated as a natural event. Markets, as much as governments, are human institutions which need careful monitoring and deliberate correction. The issue is important enough to merit elaboration.

There are many dimensions of market failure. Most text books in economics elaborate on such failures. We explain some that are cited often. First, in the absence of adequate competition, where there is monopoly (one producer) or oligopoly (few important producers), efficient market solutions characterized as optimal do not emerge. Not at least in the static world of theoretical economists. Thus, the amount of a product manufactured by a monopolist or an oligopolist may be too little and the price charged may be too high compared with competitive situations. Economists describe such situations by the phrase *imperfect markets*, to highlight the contrast with their theoretical ideal of perfect markets. Second, an economic activity may impose costs on society which are not reflected in the costs incurred by individual producers undertaking those activities, e.g. pollution caused by a chemical plant. Conversely, the activities of individual producers may create benefits for society which are not reflected in the price received by producers, e.g. skills acquired by workers in a factory. Economists characterize these effects which matter to society but are not reflected adequately in market prices (formed through individual buying or selling decisions) as *externalities*. Third, there are goods and services which are considered desirable, even essential, from the viewpoint of society. But these will not or cannot be supplied by private markets because they are not profitable enough or cannot be easily charged for, e.g. national defence and street-lights. Economists call them *public goods*. Fourth, there are goods and services which are socially desirable but individuals may not wish to pay for them even if it serves their own interests, e.g. museums or seat belts in cars. Economists coined the term *merit goods* to describe this set of goods and services. (A little reflection would show that there are close links between externalities, public goods and merit goods).

In many economic situations, where the whole is different from the sum total of the parts, market decisions may widen the divergence between private and social costs or benefits. The pursuit of profit-maximizing behaviour on the part of firms or households may lead to the over-production or overuse of goods (too many cars on the roads or too much of pesticides in agriculture), which could impose substantial costs on society in the form of environmental problems. In many instances, the atomistic pursuit of self-interest by individuals may lead to undesirable social outcomes where co-operative solutions would lead to unambiguously superior outcomes (common property rights). In so far as such market failures arise at a macro level, are discernible only over time or impose costs on society at large, they may go unnoticed by individuals or citizens who are not directly affected. (Note that pollution in big cities had to get really bad before it was taken seriously.) But the failures are for real and so are the costs they impose on society.

In this context, it is worth explaining a dimension of market failure which has received less attention than it deserves. Markets tend to underproduce information, access to which cannot be limited or priced (similar to public goods). Text books describe this as *information failure*. But it has many more facets. Markets also tend to manipulate access to information. It is not uncommon for important players in markets to supress information. Markets may even create misinformation in the pursuit of profit. The most obvious example is misleading advertising. In this day and age, when information technology is being revolutionized, probable information failure of the market deserves special attention. Unfortunately enough, it is also becoming a part of democratic politics in a market economy for all political parties to engage in such manipulation of information using the rules of the market!

There are other, perhaps even more important, market failures. At a macro level, for example, a reliance on markets often generates inflation and unemployment. Similarly, market solutions may increase poverty and inequality among people and regions. The problem is not confined to poor countries alone. There are, after all, an increasing number of homeless people on the streets of New York, just as there are an increasing number of people begging in the streets of London these days. For an economist, it is worth noting that market solutions may lead to under-investment in some sectors (where a country may even have a potential comparative advantage) or under-provision for R&D and innovation in other sectors (where technological development, again somewhat like public goods and information, is essential). It is worth considering an example that is closer to home and easier to understand. There is an emerging concern in India, even among some who are enthusiastic about economic liberalization, that there is too much portfolio investment from abroad (in the acquisition of ownership-rights in financial assets which generate income for the foreign investor) and too little direct investment from abroad (in the creation of physical assets like factories which generate employment in the economy). But this, too, is the logic of the market.

It is important to recognize that the juxtaposition of government failure and market failure, or judgements about which is worse, as if there is a choice to be made, is misleading because it diverts us into a false debate. Both market failure and government failure are facts of life. For neither markets nor governments are, or can ever be, perfect. Indeed, markets are invariably imperfect and governments are without exception fallible. The important thing is to introduce correcting devices against both market failure and government failure. These failures are seldom absolute and, except in the eyes of the dogmatist, a reasonable degree of correction is possible in either case. It is, of course, important to learn from experience but it is just as important to avoid over-reaction in learning from mistakes. Indeed, the best corrective mechanism is one which manages to avoid such swings of under-reaction and over-reaction.

Consider, for example, the erstwhile centrally planned economies of East Europe which relied almost exclusively on the State, or many developing countries where State intervention ran amuck. In both cases, there is a real danger that the reaction and the correction may go too far. In the socialist countries of yesteryears, dismantling State control and ownership hardly meant the vacuum being automatically filled by a well-functioning market. Instead, in some cases at least, it was filled by the rule of a mafia. A fact that should be obvious to any thinking person but is often lost sight of in the heat of the debate on the State versus the market is that the proper functioning of a market needs the support and, at times, the guidance of other institutions, especially that of the State. Conversely, the State cannot do without the market. In many developing countries, the withdrawal of the State from economic activity has meant an escape from bureaucratic controls. But it has also meant a liberalization of corruption, if not organized economic crime by a political mafia. India is not altogether an exception. Some captains of industry complain in private that they now pay more bribes than they did in the heyday of controls in the licence-raj. Many observers are puzzled that the process of economic liberalization may (or may not) have reduced the tyranny of the inspector-raj or babu-raj but it has certainly introduced plunders of a kickbacks-raj.

The problem arises mainly because the high priests of liberalization paint the State and the market in black and white respectively, and see the world in a binary mode. There is, however, no either-or choice to be made. On the contrary, the chances of policy failure would decrease only if we succeed in making the State and the market complement one another. Indeed, this is precisely what happens in successful market economies. As the scope of the market expands, new regulations from the State are needed which, in turn, lead to further strengthening and expansion of the market process. For instance, as the role of the market in the stock exchange expanded, or as financial instruments were created, new government regulations should have been introduced to avoid the recent financial scam in India. Such regulations would have strengthened the process of market expansion. Instead, the high priests of liberalization went on a trip of wishful thinking. They pretended that deregulation was all that was needed to release private initiative for economic development (through the stock market). It did indeed release a lot of private energy and imagination, but of the wrong kind.

II.ECONOMIC ROLE OF THE STATE

Our understanding of the role of the State in the process of development relies upon economic theory and draws upon economic history. It can be set out most simply in the form of two basic propositions. First, the State and the market are, by and large, not substitutes; instead, they must complement one another in many spheres. Second, the relationship between the State and the market cannot be specified once and for all in any dogmatic manner; instead, the two institutions must adapt to one another in a cooperative manner over time. We also believe that these propositions explain the difference between success and failure. Successful economic development is observed mostly in countries where the State and the market complement one another and adapt to one another in response to changing circumstances. This proposition is borne out both by the history of capitalism among the early industrializers during the nineteenth century and by the more recent experience of the late industrializers in the twentieth century.

Economic historians tracing the evolutionary course of the market under early capitalism noted repeatedly that the market could become the organizing principle of capitalism only when it was embedded in the regulatory mechanism of the nation state. The very extension of the scope of the free market necessitated, at each stage, the imposition of new regulations by the State to ensure further growth of the market. Thus, any characterization of the State and the market in opposition to one another is a misreading of history. Instead, it is more useful to think of the relationship as being governed by a kind of adaptive principle in which neither the State nor the market becomes destructively dominant to cripple the other institution.

In India, we must learn this historical lesson. Ironically enough, the champions of liberalization see an absolute virtue in privatization just as dogmatic leftists see an absolute virtue in nationalization! Both err in so far as they try to make one institution dominate the other in an abstract search for economic efficiency. As a result, the normal checks and balances that could develop through mutual complementarity are deliberately destroyed. The economic system is left without any mechanism of self-correction, even against gross excesses, and things go hopelessly wrong sooner or later. This is why *laissez-faire* always remained a myth rather than the reality of capitalist development. This is also why central planning in socialist economies which looked so good on paper turned out to be a failure in the longer run.

From this perspective, it is instructive to consider the experience of the late industrializers. The belief that markets know best, or that State intervention is counterproductive in the process of industrialization, is not borne out by their history. Experience from the second half of the twentieth century suggests that the guiding and supportive role of the State has been the very foundation of successful development in countries which are latecomers to industrialization. Even among the East Asian countries, which are often cited as success stories that depict the magic of the market place, the visible hand of the State is as much in evidence as the invisible hand of the market. This is the unavoidable inference if we consider, for example, the development of industrial capitalism in Japan after the Meiji Restoration in 1868 or the emergence of market socialism in China after the modernization and reform programme was launched in 1978. The economic role of the State has been almost as crucial in Korea, Taiwan and even Singapore.

In the earlier stages of industrialization, State intervention creates the conditions for the development of industrial capitalism. It creates a physical infrastructure through government investment in energy, transport and communication, which reduces the cost of inputs used by the private sector or increases the demand for goods produced by the private sector. It develops human resources through education, which raises private profitability as it lowers the private cost of training workers. It facilitates institutional change through agrarian reform, which increases productivity and incomes in the agricultural sector to foster industrialization through supply-demand linkages. We need to emphasize that institutional reform in the agricultural sector, the spread of education in society and, above all, the role of State intervention have been crucial for development among late industrializers, particularly the success stories in East Asia that are now perceived as role models. Let us not be fooled. It was not the magic of the market place which created those necessary conditions.

An important illustration of the economic role of the State in the early stages of development, among late industrializing countries, is provided by the protection of infant industries through tariffs or other means. The State protects emerging domestic entrepreneurs in the private sector from international competition in the domestic market. Thus the State and the market complement one another. If the objective is to be realized, the State must, after a time, progressively withdraw its protection so that infant industries grow up as healthy adults ultimately capable of competing in the world market. Thus the respective roles of the market and the State must undergo an adaptive change. In several developing countries, however, the objective has not been realized. There are infant industries that grow up as problem adolescents, or go from a first childhood to a second childhood without ever passing through the stage of adulthood. Such infant industries need protection for ever, in part because the paternalistic role of the State does not change adaptively over time. Even in the limited example of the infant industry argument, the difference between success and failure depends critically upon the adaptive response of State and the market to one another as circumstances and times change.

In the later stages of industrialization, it is not just the *degree* but also the *nature* of State intervention that must change. The role of the State, then, is neither that of a promoter nor that of a catalyst. The role of intervention by the State in the market can be classified conveniently as *functional, institutional* or *strategic*. Let us elaborate.

Functional intervention by the State seeks to *correct for market failures* in so far as prices give the wrong signals. It can be specific or general. That depends on the nature of the failure of the price mechanism. For example, an overnight speculative boom in the foreign exchange market, in real estate or in the stock exchange has no basis in the real economy. Such a speculative rise in prices may give wrong signals to the normal investors. Although it may be politically convenient for governments to pretend in the short-run that their liberal policies are working to generate this optimistic mood of the market, the bubble is likely to burst sooner than later. There is a strong case for early government intervention in such situations. Although, in principle, there is a case for government intervention whenever the price mechanism fails grossly, the reality is far more complex. The debate, in such cases, centres on the availability of alternative market-based solutions or the ability of governments to design and implement correct solutions on the basis of adequate information. Nevertheless, the logic of this form of intervention is, analytically, not difficult to comprehend.

Institutional intervention by the State seeks to *govern the market*. It does so by setting the rules of the game for players in the market. In particular, it creates frameworks for regulating markets and creates institutions to monitor the functioning of markets. Some examples would highlight the significance of this form of intervention. A market economy needs rules of the game to ensure a level playing field and to pre-empt a free-for-all at the same time. Thus, trade policy reform which ushers in import liberalization must be matched by a comprehensive system of anti-dumping rules for domestic firms to invoke wherever necessary. Or, the privatization of public transport requires the introduction of rules to ensure the safety of passengers and even the implementation of traffic rules to ensure the safety of pedestrians. The redline buses in the capital of India, or the mini-buses in Calcutta, operate in a market almost ungoverned by rules. They are simply allowed to maximize profits by minimizing turn-around time. In the bargain, neither pedestrians on the road nor passengers in the buses are safe. This is a 'free-for-all', not a 'level playing field'. A market economy needs regulatory legal systems to protect the rights of both entities and individuals, not merely to encourage profit at any cost. The interests of unorganized consumers are particularly important in this context. Industrial deregulation requires corresponding anti-trust laws. Financial liberalization requires matching regulatory laws. Consumer protection requires laws that curb restrictive trade practices, ensure quality control and check misinformation in advertising. A market economy needs these institutions to facilitate the function of markets. The dismantling of controls in the domestic capital market requires the equivalent of a Securities and Exchange Commission, as in the United States, that would detect trading malpractices, enforce disclosure rules and promote investor protection. The building of such an institution takes time and the Securities and Exchange Board of India has a long way to go. And it would be dishonest to pretend that the job of regulation has already been done. The privatization of public utilities which are natural monopolies—and this process has started in India with telephone services and electricity supply—requires institutions either to calibrate competition where there is a single producer or to govern pricing and protect consumers where there is more than one producer. The government also needs to protect consumers against sectional interests of many unrepresentative trade unions. While the trade union rights of workers must be respected in any genuine democracy, the government must also ensure, perhaps through secret ballot, that no unrepresentative trade union harasses ordinary consumers. Again, like in other examples, recognition of workers' rights must go with appropriate regulations for recognizing these rights. All such rules of the game need to be set transparently, and without partisanship. But, then, only a fair government can attempt to do it.

Strategic intervention by the State seeks to *guide the market*. It is interlinked across activities or sectors in an attempt to attain broader, long-term objectives of development. It is possible to cite several different types of examples. Exchange rate policy is not simply a tactical matter of getting the prices right but may turn out to be a strategic matter. Deliberately undervalued exchange rates, maintained over a period of time, have been known to provide an entry into the world market for differentiated manufactured goods. This is especially true where quality is perceived in terms of established brands but lower prices of unknown brands allow initial access to markets. Thus a strategically undervalued domestic currency makes the price of domestic manufactured exports cheaper for foreigners to buy, and gradually creates their reputation in competition with established brands. Japanese cars and cameras in an earlier period and Korean cars later may illustrate this strategy. The structure of interest rates is not just about allowing market forces to determine the scarcity price of borrowing finance, as economists are fond of saying. The structure of interest rates, short-term and long-term, may be a strategic instrument for guiding the allocation of scarce investible resources and credit in a market economy, in accordance with a long-term perspective of comparative advantage or national priorities. Restrictions on the use of foreign brand names is not symptomatic of an inward-looking attitude, if it is perceived as a strategic means of buying time to develop brand names that become acceptable in world markets after a time lag, but could never have surfaced in competition with established foreign brands. In this manner, State intervention may constitute an integral part of any strategy of industrialization that endeavours to strengthen capabilities and develop institutions rather than rely on incentives and markets alone. In these instances, strategic intervention complements rather than thwarts the initiative of domestic industrialists. This is perhaps the most important lesson that emerges from the experience of Japan and the Republic of Korea in particular, and from East Asia in general. Both Japan and Korea put exchange rate policy to such strategic use, manipulated interest rates as a strategic price to influence private investment decisions and, in effect, banned the use of foreign brands for a period of time as a strategic means of developing their own brand names. Strategic intervention by the State, particularly in the realm of industrial policy and technology policy, but also in the sphere of trade policy, rather than a blind reliance on market forces alone, has been a crucial factor underlying efficiency and dynamism in the later stages of industrialization, which enabled Japan, and then Korea, to join the league of the industrialized nations.

In India, as in East Europe, our perceptions have been so strongly influenced by the counterproductive role of State intervention in the past that we have not yet recognized the possibilities of a creative interaction between the State and the market. Hence, there is no attempt at rethinking and redefining the role of the State in India at the present stage of industrialization and development. Instead, high on rhetoric and short on thinking, our liberalizers dream of an economic miracle that would be brought about by foreign investment and multinational corporations, without the State having to play any serious economic role!

Since we do not rely on miracles, our rethinking must recognize the complementarity between the State and the market. The relationship must be characterized by co-operation, not conflict. It must also evolve with time. Given that the entrepreneurial talents of the private sector and the capabilities of the State, as also the needs of economy and society, change over time, this relationship must be flexible and adaptive. The crux of the problem is to assess the costs of government failure and market failure at critical points of time, so as to minimize the cost to society. And those who never tire of emphasizing the costs of State intervention must also recognize the costs of State inaction at such critical points. In the present context, therefore, we need to reformulate the questions about the economic role of the State. The real question is no longer about the size of the State (how big?) or the degree of State intervention (how much?). The question is now about the nature of State intervention (what sort?) and the quality of the performance of the State (how good?).

In our view, the respective roles of the government and the market or the public sector and the private sector should be determined by the comparative advantage of each. There can be no hard and fast rules, for boundaries change over time as comparative advantage or circumstances change. But there are some things

141

which are best left to private initiative. There are other things which should remain responsibilities of the government. There are yet other things in which the private and public sectors need to co-exist and compete. Let a few examples suffice to illustrate. Governments should not run hotels or produce textiles in the public sector. Such economic activities are more sensibly left to the private sector. As a general principle, with some exceptions, final goods and services sold to a large number of consumers, which are not natural monopolies and where there are no prohibitive scale economies, should be in the domain of the private sector with one important proviso: *competition*. Government regulations alone cannot ensure quality at reasonable prices. We know that from experience. But quality can be maintained through competition among producers. As long as there are some producers in each area, consumers would have a choice. The role of the government in such sectors is to ensure that producers in the private sector do not enter into implicit agreements, or form cartels, that would jeopordize consumer interests. On the other hand, public utilities which are natural monopolies, say the railways, should remain in the public sector, because competition in the form of more producers is uneconomic if it means a wasteful duplication of tracks or stations; moreover, private ownership would reduce or skew the availability of services to users if it invests in or develops the high-density routes but neglects or closes down low-density routes. In some sectors, however, there is no reason why the public sector and the private sector should not co-exist, for competition would keep both on their toes. This is particularly important where market structures are oligopolistic because the importance of scale economies limits the number of producers, as in steel or petrochemicals. The same reasoning can be extended to civil aviation where the entry of a few private airlines has provided much needed competition to the public sector.

In considering any division of labour between the public sector and the private sector, it is important to stress two points. First, there is no unambiguous relationship between ownership and performance. It is motivated ideology, rather than fact, which leads liberalizers to suggest that private ownership always means good performance and public ownership always means bad performance. We would do well to remember that Pan American, a private airline, went bankrupt in the heartland of capitalism, while Singapore Airlines, entirely State-owned, is among the best. Such examples abound. The economic efficiency of an enterprise is determined more by competition in the market structure and competence (together with accountability) in the management than by the nature of its ownership. Second, the comparative advantage of the public sector and the private sector not only differs across sectors but also changes over time. Thus, the respective domains of the public sector and the private sector in the economy must also evolve and adapt in much the same way as the relationship between the State and the market.

In a country such as India, the relative economic role of the State as a producer should diminish over time. At the present stage of development, however, the government must continue, and not abandon, its efforts to develop the physical infrastructure, just as it must strengthen, and not dilute, its role in creating a social infrastructure. It must not abandon its efforts and dilute its role in the name of liberalization. This is absolutely essential if we want the economic priorities of the people to merge into the development objectives of the nation. At the same time, particularly in India, the government must endeavour to change the nature and the quality of its intervention in the market, consciously differentiating between the functional, the institutional and the strategic aspects. Their impact would be felt over different time horizons. But the government simply cannot afford to abdicate its role in the belief that markets know best or under the illusion that foreign investment would do the trick. It is only a creative cooperation between the

State and the market, which evolves adaptively over time, that can foster rapid economic development in India. The 'State-market debate' can be meaningful only on these terms.

III. POLITICS AND THE NATURE OF THE STATE

We have argued that it is both necessary and desirable to redefine the role of the State in India at the present juncture. We also believe that the economic role of the State in India would continue to be important for some time to come, even as the scope of the market increases through liberalization. Most people, we think, will find our arguments persuasive, if not obvious. But many will doubt whether this redefined economic role for the State is feasible in India in terms of politics. The reason for scepticism is understandable given the existing nature of our politics. The willingness and the ability of the State to perform such a role depends on the nature of the State. It also depends on the agenda of the State. Both are, in turn, shaped by the underlying politics. The recent experience of India provides less and less hope for optimism. But must we enter Dante's Hell abandoning all hope ?

The nature of the State in India (as also its actual agenda) has been shaped by the class structure of society overlapping with the divides of caste and religion, on the one hand, and the compulsions of electoral politics in the most poor and populous democracy in the world, on the other. The pronounced social and economic inequalities have, inevitably, meant an unequal distribution of political power. Hence, by and large, the State has represented the interests of the dominant economic and social classes that constitute the ruling elite. This reality has been moderated by the compulsions of a democracy where governments are elected by the people and where the vast majority of the people are poor. The mandate to rule has to be renewed at least once in five years. Winning elections depends upon getting votes from the poor. This is an important fact of political life which distinguishes India from many other developing countries. It is a fact which cannot be ignored by politicians. The distribution of votes, unlike the distribution of incomes or assets, is equal. One adult has one vote in politics, even though a rich man has more 'votes' than a poor man, in terms of purchasing power, in the market. Thus, the State in India needs political legitimation from the people, most of whom are poor.

In principle, these conflicting pressures of economics and politics on the State could have been used to provide a healthy system of checks and balances, in the form of different self-correcting mechanisms which are the essence of democracy. In practice, however, it has meant the worst of both worlds. The vested interests of the dominant classes or the elite have perpetuated a cynical politics of soft options, while the State has shied away from hard decisions. It is both unwilling and unable to tread on the toes of the rich and the powerful. At the same time, the need for legitimation from the people, particularly the support of the underprivileged or the poor, has bred a competitive politics of populism. Political parties have sought to woo the people with sops especially around election time. 'Left' or 'right' no longer matters in this game. There is a hypocrisy in this process which is nauseating. The relationship between the State and the industrial capitalist class in India has been antagonistic on the surface, operating through a maze of controls, but has been symbiotic beneath the surface, operating through a maze of corruption. The relationship between the State and the poor has been close in terms of rhetoric, voiced through catchy slogans about poverty eradication (*garibi hatao*) or affirmative action (reservations in jobs) or class struggle (power to the people), but it has been distant in terms of reality. The undeniable evidence is that hundreds of millions of people are unable to meet basic needs such as food and clothing despite five decades of repeated promises. It is worth stressing that, in this respect, there is not much difference between the centre, where one party has ruled for most of the time, and the states, where different parties have ruled at different times. The hypocritical politics of populism seems to be the great equalizer of political parties in India !

The State has, thus, provided a means of sharing the spoils in conformity with the dictates of politics. Populism has been a part of this process. The system prospered for a time, and then survived, because there has been almost no transparency or accountability. The passage of time has, however, increasingly strained the system and brought it into disrepute. Over the past three decades, the people have brought down governments through the electoral process, to begin with in the states and later at the centre, to convey their unhappiness or vent their anger, only to find that the more things change the more they remain the same. As a result, there is now widespread disillusionment among the people with political parties irrespective of ideology and political leaders and unmindful of personality. The credibility of the government and of the State is now low in the eyes of the citizens. The truth of the old maxim that 'you can fool all of the people for some of the time or some of the people for all of the time but you cannot fool all of the people for all of the time' describes the political reality in India.

Economic liberalization has been introduced in such a milieu, while there has been no change in the nature of the State or in the nature of politics in India. It should come as no surprise that the proposed escape from bureaucratic controls has led to a liberalization of corruption. It has neither unshackled the elephant nor uncaged the tiger. Instead, it may well have let loose a bunch of corrupt politicians and bureaucrats on the people. We have simply moved from an old world of licences or permits to a new world of percentages or kickbacks, for the neta-babu raj has remained the same. This raj is no less adept at corrupting market forces than it was at corrupting State intervention. That is the lesson to learn.

It must be said clearly, with all the force at our command, that a State which fails in intervention is also bound to fail in liberalization. For the same reason, a State that cannot run enterprises cannot regulate, let alone govern or guide, markets. Therefore, if nothing changes in the realm of politics nothing will change in the sphere of economics. It will continue to be business-as-usual. The netas and babus will do much the same with or without liberalization.

There is, at present, widespread gloom about the state of politics in India. We believe that there is reason for pessimism about the future but not for gloom. And we must not give up hope. For if politics is the art of the possible, change is in the domain of the feasible. The reader may, naturally, be curious about our view of the State which holds out this glimmer of hope. It hardly needs to be said that the State in India is not made up of Plato's guardians. However, despite the emerging nexus between politics and crime, we do not think that the State in India is run by the equivalent of an organized Sicilian mafia. Or at least not as yet. The nature of the State in India is roughly what you would expect in an economy, polity and society that is characterized by diverse forms of inequalities. The reality is much too complex to be capsuled in terms of conventional analytical categories at either end of the ideological spectrum. For India is a society in which different cultures (traditional and modern), different divides (caste, class and religion) or even different centuries (nineteenth—if not the middle ages -and twentieth) co-exist. In such a diverse context, we need have neither an *idealistic* view of the State nor a *fatalistic* view of the State. We would suggest a *realistic* view of the State, which recognizes the many revealed weaknesses of the system but does not ignore the possibilities of exploiting the few potential strengths still left in the system. The weaknesses and the strengths are both mingled with India's overwhelming diversity.

The paramount strength of the system is democracy. India is among the very few developing countries where democracy has taken deep roots in polity and society. It is only because of democracy that India continues as one country despite such diversity. In a democracy, there exist checks and balances which could make it possible to exercise an influence on the nature of the State and the nature of politics. The much needed change in politics is feasible if—and only if—we can introduce *transparency* and *accountability* into the system. That is what meaningful democracy is about, for it creates self-correcting mechanisms which are capable of learning from mistakes. Transparency is necessary but not sufficient. It must be combined with accountability. But transparency must come first, because there can be no accountability without transparency.

There is little transparency in our political system. Indeed, there never has been. The citizen would be justified in coming to the conclusion that we have to wait for a scandal to surface before information is provided. And nothing has changed since the advent of liberalization. Is it not strange that we need a scandal every time to elicit information from the government about liberalization? The experience repeats itself time after time and with distressing fequency—the stock scam, the Enron deal, the MS Shoes fiasco, the Bailadila mine episode—and we can easily multiply these examples. Every time information has to be cajoled, squeezed or forced out of a reluctant government by parliamentary committees or a persistent press. But that is not all. It is even more strange that the executive does not share information with parliament in the business of governance. Liberalization, which can be sustained only through open political support in a democracy, is introduced almost by stealth. Economic refroms come through the promulgation of ordinances soon after parliament has adjourned, or just before it is convened, rather than through an open debate in parliament followed by an enactment of legislation! The most striking example is that of the amendment of the patents law which ultimately met with a filibuster in the Rajya Sabha. Understandably, the lack of transparency on the part of the government succeeds only in arousing suspicion, not support. This is illustrated most clearly by the government's reluctance to share its assessment of the results of the Uruguay Round of multilateral trade negotiations, with the parliament or the people, to allow some time for public debate before the acceptance of substantial international obligations. It only led to speculation and allegations that the government was compromising the national interest, perhaps in pursuit of a hidden agenda.

The story does not end here. It extends even to situations where the government has little to hide or nothing to fear from public scrutiny. The reluctance to share information has become an almost natural instinct. It may not be common knowledge, but the perception inside the government is that the most able civil servants and ministers are those who divulge the minimum information in response to questions in parliament. There are many variations around this theme. Information is not disclosed as a rule. Information is withheld even when asked for, by invoking secrecy laws or, ironically enough, by claiming that it would not be in the public interest. Information provided on a selective basis often misleads. It conceals more than it reveals. Information is closely held and manipulated, as a source of power, by a privileged few inside the government. The more dishonest among them frequently use it for personal economic or policical gain, but almost everybody considered influential shares in restricting information for exercising power. The object of the exercise is to suit the convenience of the government in power, not to serve the interests of the people.

Similarly, there is almost no accountability in government. What little there was has disappeared with the passage of time. It would seem that individuals in public office are no longer accountable for impropriety, wrongdoing or dishonesty on their part. You can never be sure how much you know because there is no transparency. You can only suspect. Politicians who went into oblivion because they were known to be corrupt are rehabilitated as ministers in government with portfolios that are known to be lucrative. Ministers who are indicted by some form of public scrutiny continue unashamedly in office and cannot be dropped or forced to resign. Some political leaders become powerful in the system because they have largesse to disburse. Much the same is true of civil servants. The incidence of corruption has grown rapidly, much beyond the proverbial chaprasi, babu or inspector to the highest level in the civil service system. Yet, it is rare for a civil servant to be punished, leave alone dismissed, for corruption. The corrupt and the pliant prosper as the system rewards them only for loyalty to the master. Those who do not want to buck the system and look the other way manage to survive. But the few who are both honest and competent are seldom rewarded. Indeed, some of them are even penalized if their integrity or their ability is perceived as an inconvenience or a hurdle. The system, when pushed, finds some sacrificial lambs for the altar (who are often no more than petty functionaries), but these are exceptions that prove the rule.

Any notion of accountability, which is based entirely on corruption or immorality, is much too narrow. In any democracy, individuals and institutions are also accountable for the consequences of their actions in the discharge of their public responsibilities. But this accountability has almost vanished in India.

When things go wrong, it is described as a 'systems failure'. As if God created the system and no human being can be held responsible for its failure. Neither ministers nor civil servants are held responsible when things go wrong under their supervision. Recall, for example, the financial scam of 1992 which was by far the biggest financial scandal in independent India. As the disturbing sequence of developments unfolded, the Finance Minister made the following statement in Parliament: 'But that does not mean that I should lose my sleep simply because the stock market goes up one day and falls the next day' (quoted in the Report of the Joint Parliamentary Committee to Enquire into Irregularities in Securities and Banking Transactions, Lok Sabha Secretariat, December 1993, Volume I, p.211). This led the parliamentary committee, which enquired into the scam, to observe : 'It is good to have a Finance Minister who does not lose his sleep easily but one would wish that when such cataclysmic changes take place all around some alarm would ring to disturb his slumber' (*ibid*, p.211). The minister, as is the norm in any parliamentary system, was accountable in the sense of constructive responsibility. The importance of this principle was also emphasized by the parliamentary committee which concluded that 'the responsibility and accountability of the Finance Minister to parliament cannot be denied' (*ibid*, p.223). But this was ignored by the government. It is another matter that ministers have resigned and officials have been indicted in the wake of similar scandals in other countries. Or, consider the example of a sequence of air crashes or railway accidents. The ministers for civil aviation or the railways are not directly culpable but are again accountable in the sense of constructive responsibility. It was not so long ago, even in India, that ministers resigned following such events. Unfortunately, this is no longer so.

In this milieu, it is hardly surprising that ministers and civil servants are not accountable for the outcome of policies adopted during their tenure. There is an irony about the transition from the *dirigisme* of the past to the economic liberalization of the present that may have escaped attention. It may be odd but there is no change in the *dramatis personae*. The architects of what is now described as excessive and inappropriate State intervention of the

151

past changed colours. As the high-priests of economic liberalization, they now preach to us about the sins we committed and the need for reform. In most countries, whether in the industrialized world or in the developing world, such a change in policies would almost certainly have meant a change of persons. This, too, is possible in India only because of the absence of accountability.

We would like to emphasize again that accountability is not simply, or even primarily, a moral issue in the context of economic liberalization. It has many implications at more mundane levels. Consider, for example, accountability for the poor performance or the low profitability of public sector enterprises. The reason why the debate sounds hollow is straightforward. We cannot expect to hold public sector workers or management accountable, or punishable, with any conviction when the minister or bureaucrats in charge are not seen to be accountable, in any way, by the public. To be convincing, accountability must begin from the top and not from the bottom. Similarly, the 'indiscipline' of workers and trade unions, that our architects of liberalization frequently lament about, can be dealt with only if the same standards of rigour are applied to politicians and bureaucrats (as also their godmen) in high places.

The Indian media has, in a sense, been an insurance if not a saving grace of the system. It has provided some checks and balances. Many scandals have been exposed by investigative journalism. Reports in newspapers have induced debates in parliament. Writing in the media has introduced some notion of accountability in the public eye, which has played a vital role around election time. But there are limits to this process which must be recognized. For one, the media is sometimes influenced by the intimidation of the State and often co-opted by the patronage of the State; the latter is happening more and more. For another, public memory is short and newspapers come out every morning. The scandals of yesterday are overtaken by the disasters of today. What is more, the print media can only reach out to those who are literate. The electronic media, which has a wide reach and a powerful influence, is more or less captive of the government and even satellite television is not immune as control is exercised in a variety of ways. Again, the direct and indirect control over the electronic media, exercised by the government, erodes transparency and diminishes accountability further. What is the economic argument our liberalizers would give for so much government control of the electronic media ?

It should be obvious that transparency and accountability which has to be extracted inch by inch from an unwilling government is simply not enough. A change in the nature of politics is feasible only with the introduction of genuine transparency and accountability in our system. Such transparency and accountability must begin with the government and the State for it can be enforced in a democracy. In the pursuit of transparency, we must move from secrecy to openness in government so that the disclosure of information is the rule and not the exception. Information should be made available by the government not only to the parliament and the media but also to the interested citizens. And there should be no holy-cows, not even defence expenditure, that are exempted from public scrutiny. In the realm of accountability, the most important thing is the creation of ombudsman-like institutions at every level which can investigate charges of corruption against those in government. The guilty must be punished and justice must be seen to be done. It is the only means of restoring credibility of our political system in the eyes of the people. But that cannot be enough. Ministers and civil servants must learn to be accountable, in terms of constructive responsibility, when things go wrong under their supervision or during their tenure. Accountability would ultimately mean that there are rewards for integrity and ability, combined with penalties for dishonesty or incompetence, in public life. This would slowly but surely change the culture of politics.

It is important to emphasize that the nature of politics can be changed in a sustainable manner if these principles of transparency and accountability are extended beyond the government to political parties. The Indian experience so far suggests that transparency is not convenient for any political party because it brings with it the threat of accountability. Hence, there is a conspiracy of silence on the agenda for political reform. To start with, transparency requires a complete disclosure of contributions received and expenditures incurred by political parties in the form of audited accounts available for public scrutiny. This process may be helped by a partial public funding of elections and more realistic ceilings on electoral campaign expenditure. At another, more important level, transparency needs honest sharing of information with the electorate. The manifestos of political parties must, therefore, say what they mean and mean what they say, rather than posture before the elections only to change their stance after the event. Ideology, then, is an important point of reference, which can curb even if not pre-empt political opportunism, because transparency in this form carries with it at least some accountability.

We are hopeful that it is possible to change both the culture and the nature of politics in India. In this quest, the introduction of transparency and accountability in our political system is only a beginning, for it is necessary but cannot be sufficient. But a beginning can be made now. There are two reasons underlying our optimism. First, we are in transition from a political system in which there was one dominant political party to a political system in which there will be, on present reckoning, three political formations at the national level and many more at the state level. Political parties in opposition, when out of power, have a lower stake in keeping the system devoid of transparency and accountability. Political parties in coalition, when in power, have a higher stake in transparency and accountability, at least vis-a-vis each other for that can be the only basis of a stable coalition. The era of opposition politics and coalition politics could therefore set the stage for a necessary beginning. This process could gather momentum as it captures the popular imagination. Second, in the five decades since independence, democracy has taken roots at the level of the common people in polity and society. There may be widespread disillusionment but there is also a political consciousness among voters, who judge political parties and their performance. It is possible to discern some evidence of an increasing, almost silent, participation and mobilization by the people in the democratic process. And, in the ultimate analysis, it is the sanction and the will of the people that will provide the self-correcting mechanisms to our democracy. This process takes time. In the interim, the introduction of transparency and accountability is the most significant battle in the arena of politics for winning the war of India's economic development. Reform and change must begin there.

Chapter 6

Sensible Economics and Feasible Politics

There is a Buddhist proverb which captures, in some ways, the essence of the problem of economic liberalization in a vast, poor country like India. 'The key to the gate of Heaven,' goes the proverb, 'is also the key which could open the gate to hell.' Indeed, danger and opportunity are so intricately intermingled in the liberalization of the Indian economy that the journey to the promised land of a well-functioning market economy could easily turn into a hellish nightmare of poverty and widening inequality for the majority. It is fortunate that we have a democratic set-up and a relatively free press. These institutions may not be most 'efficient' for pursuing economic policies with a single-minded purpose, but they can correct excesses when the journey to prosperity through the market turns into a stock exchange 'scam' or an underhand deal with a multinational corporation and, in a wider context, increases economic deprivation or social alienation. It is this institutional framework of a political democracy that we must learn to respect and devise economic policies in that context. This chapter explores how we can blend sensible economics with feasible politics in India. In doing so, it addresses four questions. How would the people of India judge economic liberalization or, for that matter, any strategy of development? What needs to be done by the government and how should we assess its economic performance with reference to these re-oriented objectives? Why are the long term issues in development so different from the almost trivial pursuits of the present architects of economic liberalization? Finally, how can we turn the strength of our political democracy into the driving force for India's economic development?

I. A LITMUS TEST

We believe that liberalization must be considered not only in the light of what is desirable in the abstract from an economic point of view, but also with reference to what is feasible in the concrete from a political perspective. The political feasibility of economic liberalization has a simple test in Indian democracy. It must alleviate the problems which make day to day life so difficult for the average citizen of India. In other words, liberalization would be tested not in terms of some abstract principles, but in terms of tangible results it yields to improve the living conditions or the daily existence of ordinary people. And it is precisely in this respect that both the left wing critics as well as the right wing enthusiasts of liberalization have often gone wrong. For instance, a common mistake of the left rhetoric is to criticize economic liberalization in terms of such abstract criteria as the erosion of 'national economic sovereignty'. Such political slogans based on abstract rhetoric do not directly address important questions like unemployment, inflation and poverty. The link between 'economic sovereignty' and these basic problems is far from clear to anybody. Similarly, the mistake of the right enthusiasts is to hide increasingly behind a smoke-screen of economic technicalities. They stress the comfortable balance of payments situation, the stability of the rupee in foreign exchange markets and the supposed control over government deficits.

The common man or woman is not taken in by catchy slogans or mystifying jargon. For that matter, any responsible politician answerable to his or her constituency need not, and should not be bother with any such smoke-screen of technicalities. He or she must learn to judge the performance of liberalization in terms of its impact on the day to day problems of economic existence. And if politicians fail to appreciate this ground reality, popular verdicts in elections will teach them that necessary lesson. The bottom line is simple enough. If liberalization cannot give drinking water, irrigation and electricity to the villages of India, primary education and basic health care to the people, or employment to the unemployed and the poor, it will not be taken seriously irrespective of the technical mumbo-jumbo. It is a sad comment on the current state of the Indian debate that populist rhetoric, either emphasizing the loss of 'national economic sovereignty' or glorifying the 'magic of the market' and the 'wonders of globalization', tends to cloud our judgement. The performance of these policies with respect to concrete issues like poverty and unemployment or education and health care is seldom debated seriously.

The enthusiasts for liberalization often pretend that these basic problems of development will be solved over time through austerity practised by the government coupled with the creation of a favourable climate for foreign investment. The critics of liberalization, especially the traditional left, used to be sceptical of such reasoning and rightly so. But their own performance, in terms of precisely these concrete issues of daily existence, has been almost as dismal in parts of India where they are in power. So they now try to differentiate their product for electoral purposes. In effect, however, they have also come to rely on investment by multinational corporations as the saviour. They seem incapable of implementing any other strategy of development. It would appear that we are living in a land of the eyeless where 'left' and 'right' no longer give directions to economic policy.

The fundamental issue, however, is not so complicated. Whether economic liberalization or not, a range of basic economic problems faced by the average Indian has to be solved speedily, by whatever means. Moreover, this has to be compatible with our political structure of democracy and federalism. In that sense, desirable economics and feasible politics are two sides of the same coin. The problems can be solved only if we get our economic priorities right. Economic policies must reflect the priorities which an average citizen attaches to the problems he or she faces every day. More simply, this means that the proverbial common man or woman must feel that liberalization is helping to solve his or her day to day problems of existence. There is so much nervousness about the future course of liberalization precisely because this has not happened. Juggling with statistics, speeches in parliament, conventions in five-star hotels or visits by foreign dignitaries should not blind us to this most powerful and elementary of criteria in a democracy.

Any economic policy—liberalization or something else—will automatically become feasible politics, and generate enthusiasm and popular support when it achieves this. The problem with the current programme of liberalization, as it is being pursued, lies precisely here. When the process of economic liberalization began in 1991, we were told (in accordance with the IMF mantra) that austerity is needed in economy and society, especially in the government, for a more prosperous future. The future remains very much in the future. However, with elections around the corner, populist measures have to be promised in an attempt to get votes, although even a fool knows that such populist measures cannot be sustainable. This is neither feasible economics nor desirable politics.

Indeed, we should have had the courage to say to the IMF from the beginning of liberalization that the average standard of living must improve here and now, if these policies are to be sustainable in a democracy. 'Austerity now, for prosperity later' is a false start in every way. In particular, we need not wait for either the

162

multinational corporations or the non-resident Indians to deliver us to the promised land of prosperity, while the practice of austerity hurts mainly the poor. Nor do we require the Prime Minister, Chief Ministers or Finance Ministers to make regular trips abroad in pathetic attempts to attract direct foreign investment. Instead, they need to do their job seriously at home, which is to ensure that living standards of our people improve steadily with or without foreign capital inflows. We argue that this is economically feasible, and that is the line of action we must pursue.

The main economic thrust must be to force the central government and the state governments to take the sort of responsibility which they have now more or less abdicated in the name of liberalization. Governments at all levels must realize that foreign investment will neither be attracted nor is it worth having, unless a basic economic, social and legal infrastructure is provided by the government. A government that cannot manage the social infrastructure—primary education, health care, housing or even drinking water—and the physical infrastructure—transport, power or communications—cannot solve the economic problems of the people in any case, with or without foreign investment. There are, for instance, quite a few countries in Latin America which received large amounts of foreign investment in the aggregate and in per capita terms, but are no better for that. Multinationals or foreigners cannot and will not do the job which governments are supposed to do.

II. ASSESSING ECONOMIC PERFORMANCE OF THE GOVERNMENT

The usual objection will be raised, especially by those who advocate liberalization, that 'the government has no money'. This, we submit, is both bad economics and bad politics when viewed in this context. John Maynard Keynes, the greatest economist of this

163

century, revolutionized our thinking in economics by explaining why the management of public finance is qualititatively different from that of private or individual finance. Without going into that specific doctrine, which claimed that government spending could be self-financing in some situations, and its validity in developing countries, let it suffice to mention here that large government spending will be absolutely essential in India if the government has to face and to discharge its responsibilities. What is more, the government must not shy away from deficit spending when it is genuinely needed for development. As we have repeatedly pointed out in this book, blanket austerity on government finance, IMF style, which is in favour with the powers that be does not have any intellectual validity in terms of economic theory. The problem is not to reduce government spending, including deficit spending, but to hold the government accountable for spending productively. This is because government spending is sustainable so long as it is sufficiently productive.

We would like to emphasize that large scale government spending, even if a part of it is based on deficit financing or borrowing from the public, will be non-inflationary and sustainable if the three following criteria are satisfied. First, the real rate of growth of the economy must be greater than the real rate of interest at which the government borrows. The real rate in both cases is obtained by correcting the growth in the GDP at current market prices, and the nominal interest rate, for the rate of inflation. Second, the favourable impact of government spending needs to be felt in improved basic economic and social infrastructural facilities, which raises social consumption to generate popular support. This will not only lend political feasibility to the programme, but will also create the stable and optimistic environment essential for economic development. Third, the government must show itself as capable not only in terms of spending effectively, but also in terms of mobilizing resources (through tax and non-tax revenues) effectively. This requires that government revenue collection 'at the margin', out of *increased* income in the economy, must exceed government spending out of the same increased income. It is necessary to elaborate a little on these three criteria we have enunciated. To begin with, consider the first criterion that the rate of growth of the economy in real terms must be higher than the rate of interest in real terms. This necessarily implies that government expenditure must be sufficiently productive to generate high growth. In turn, this means four things.

(a) The government must be able to shift its spending from consumption to productive investment. This goes against the soft option of populism and no government, right or left, has so far been serious about it. However, we must remember that we have no right to reject IMF-style austerity in public finance, unless we can shift the composition of government expenditure steadily from consumption (e.g. increased salaries and bonuses for government employees or more subsidies for groups whom the government seeks to benefit or placate) to investment. If this requires an explicit 'incomes policy' and some stated principle of parity between salaries in the private and public sector, or if this requires a transparent assessment of hidden subsidies, it must be openly debated as a part of liberalization.

(b) The government must direct public investment into the creation and development of a physical infrastructure for the economy, in particular power, transport and communications. The withdrawal of the government from these sectors is premature because sufficient private investment, whether domestic or foreign, is not forthcoming, at least not so far, perhaps because of the high risks, the long gestation lags or the sheer size of the investment needed. In fact, experience from elsewhere in the developing world—and even some industrialized countries such as the United Kingdom—suggests that the private sector simply does not and cannot make the requisite investment in infrastructure. We must learn from this concrete experience instead of being captivated by slogans about privatization. In India, the returns on such investment by the government would not be confined to these sectors alone but would accrue across the board in the economy, as the infrastructure created would ease supply bottlenecks which constrain production and distribution. This expenditure would thus raise the rate of growth of the economy.

(c) The government must have the courage to face the fact that defence expenditure must be reduced because this is the most significant form of unproductive government expenditure in terms of the repayment of public debt. Yet, no political party is willing to even debate the issue openly. It is our opinion that, no matter what our position is on Kashmir or on the geo-political perspective of the region or on the threat of terrorism, the best form of defence is to have a popular government which can mobilize the support of an overwhelming majority in its favour whenever need arises. These threats loom large precisely because our economic performance has been so uneven and unsatisfactory. We only need to compare India with some countries in south-east Asia, such as Malaysia, which used to be torn by ethnic tensions some years ago. Satisfactory economic performance reduced that tension. Much like our 'forced liberalization' of 1991 (see Chapter 2), militarism is at best a crisis-driven response which must be complemented by a longer term strategy of development.

(d) The use and the cost of borrowing by the government to finance the spending is absolutely crucial. The government must not borrow to finance its consumption expenditure, for such spending yields no returns. Indeed, the revenue deficit of the government must be progressively reduced and rapidly eliminated. Similarly, the (average) interest rate at which the government borrows is an important consideration because a higher interest rate in real terms only means that, in terms of our criterion, the rate of growth of the economy in real terms would have to be even higher. Thus, there is no virtue in eliminating (altogether) low-cost borrowing from the Reserve Bank of India in the belief that the associated monetary expansion would cause inflation, or in raising (significantly) the interest rates on government securities in the belief that borrowing at market prices would make the government more responsible. It is imperative that we introduce the necessary correctives.

In addition to the above, raising the productivity of public expenditure requires a meaningful restructuring of the public sector to raise its efficiency and productivity. Much as this deserves a very high priority in any programme of economic reforms, there is precious little that has been done in concrete terms. In this task, we must be wary of the rhetoric, both on the right and on the left.

Those on the right parrot slogans of privatization. This does not mean anything. In any case, as we have explained earlier, the sale of government equity in public sector enterprises, by itself, serves little purpose. In terms of macro-economic management, it would be far more desirable to use capital receipts from such disinvestment to retire public debt, rather than to reduce the fiscal deficit of the government. From the perspective of the public sector, it would be preferable to use proceeds from the sale of government equity, at least in part, to restructure public enterprises. It must also be recognized that there is no unique relationship between ownership and performance. The efficiency of an enterprise is determined more by competition in the market structure and by competence in the management than by the nature of its ownership. Thus, it is essential to expose public sector firms to competition in the market. Similarly, it is crucial to provide the management of public sector enterprises with an *autonomy* and follow it up with an *accountability*. There is nothing intrinsic which makes managers in the public sector worse and managers in the private sector better. The real problem is that, so far public enterprises neither enjoy autonomy nor are held accountable. The public sector has been treated instead as the goose that lays the golden eggs for the governmental system.

Those on the left do not tire of voicing their concern about workers' interests. We need to realize that trade union interest in the public sector, irrespective of which particular political party controls it, is a sectional interest. More often than not, it does not serve the interest of the working people or of economic development in general. Trade unions must become economically responsible. For this, we may apply a simple criterion. We should give selected public sector enterprises, that are not of strategic importance, the same degree of freedom from the government bureaucracy as to the private sector firms. However, in all branches of industry and trade where such public and private sector enterprises co-exist, if the public enterprises continue to make operating losses while their counterparts in the private sector do not, those public sector firms must be forced to fend for themselves. Recent experience in civil aviation, hotels and road transport comes readily to mind. Without such discipline imposed on the public sector, we cannot satisfy the criterion that the real rate of growth of production in the economy through sufficiently high productivity of government expenditure must exceed the real rate of interest at which the government borrows.

It needs to be stressed that such discipline can be imposed on public sector trade unions only if the criterion of accountability is followed all along at higher levels. It is not only the management that must be accountable, but also their higher authorities in the government who must be accountable. When neither the head of a central bank nor a finance minister are accountable for the largest financial scam this country has ever seen, how can we hold trade unions responsible for loss-making public sector enterprises? Accountability can be enhanced also by setting voluntary examples. Any minister who makes foreign trips on public money every summer for attracting foreign investment, just as much as the countless government delegations who escape the summer heat of Delhi to propogate the cause of liberalization in the West, need to hold himself, or themselves, accountable to the public by stating transparently how effective such expenditure of public money has actually been. Like charity, discipline begins at home, and at the highest levels.

If accountability based on transparency of information is one way to fight populism which continuously makes public expenditure unproductive, the other major way to counter populism is to ensure a steady improvement in the economic well-being of the ordinary Indian. This does not require a sharp increase in wages and salaries which all populist governments are prone to do. Instead, governments must work to provide a steady and systematic increase in *social* consumption, which is our second criterion. Social consumption consists of access to basic education (primary and secondary), basic health care which includes clean drinking water, preventive health and public hygiene, child and mother care, family planning and similar social services. It also includes provision for housing and sanitation. We differ from received orthodoxy and claim that the government in India must be willing to spend massively on these programmes of social infrastructure.

In particular, we suggest four areas where public expenditure and its reorientation is particularly desirable. This is based in part on our judgement and in part on research carried out by other economists. First, fertilizer subsidies should be cut but that expenditure should be reallocated for public investment in irrigation. Many econometric exercises show that this would be most desirable. What is more, populist rhetoric cannot label it as anti-peasant or anti-agriculture. Second, in the sphere of human resource development, a time-bound programme of primary education for *all* (especially girls) must receive the highest priority. There should be no excuses about the lack of funds. It must be done here and now. In the short-term, if necessary, funds should be reoriented within the education budget with more private funding as a supplement for higher education. But there is a strong case for stepping up the resources made available for education not only in real terms but also as a proportion of GDP. Third, there should be a crash programme to provide safe drinking water for the people, particularly in rural areas, but also in urban areas. It is a shame that after almost five decades since independence, India is unable to provide drinking water to a large segment of its population. The resources needed for this purpose are not by any means enormous. These must be set aside and the implementation must begin now on a time-bound basis. This is not just social consumption. There can be no better investment in public health. Fourth, public housing and toilets should be built on a massive scale, especially in smaller towns where land is still available. These houses should be sold on easy instalments, and the government must place orders for building materials and their transport, utilizing fully existing capacities, say in the cement or wagon industry. Lack of money is a bad economic excuse insofar as excess capacity exists in cement and other building industries. We are told that in South Korea the poorest (like street-dwellers in our big cities) were given physical building materials and engineering help to build their own houses. Eviction can be morally justified only if people are not willing to help themselves in this manner.

These are four crucial examples of how public expenditure can help to increase both productivity and social consumption. This would, at the same time, create a sense of social consensus for economic policy. Ours is not a romantic programme, but feasible politics for desirable economics in India. It will be sustainable so long as our three criteria for public expenditure are broadly satisfied. In terms of politics, it requires the accountability of the government at all levels when it fails to carry out its expenditure and investment properly. The information required for this can be obtained through technical expert committees in various fields, which need to remain outside the government bureaucracy. They could place regular reports before the parliament and the press on issues of public concern, particularly those relating to social consumption. It must be realized that the people of India have the right to know how the government is performing. They also have the right to criticize, not every five years, just before elections, but say every six months on the basis of information provided by independent experts who do not belong to any political party.

Long-term public expenditure to improve productivity, without the populism of soft options, is our only path to development. Liberalization must be founded on this, and not on austerity. Moreover, social consensus achieved not through austerity but through a steady increase in social consumption would provide a degree of political stability, which is also an economic asset for any government, even for attracting foreign investors. Let it suffice here to say that the somewhat artificial stability of the rupee maintained by attracting deposits from non-resident Indians, or portfolio investment from foreign institutional investors, is no substitute for such genuine political and economic stability. High interest rates even make the viability of large public expenditure (including deficit financing) more problematic insofar as the task of ensuring that the real growth rate exceeds the real interest rate becomes all the more difficult.

The third criterion we had mentioned earlier for sustainability of government expenditure spells out the precise fiscal responsibility of the government. Unlike the IMF, we do not believe that fiscal responsibility comes from any analytically groundless criteria such as an upper limit on the fiscal deficit (total borrowing by the government), say, at 5 per cent of GDP, or an elimination of the monetized deficit (borrowing from the central bank). Such criteria have no basis in theory. As we have mentioned earlier, any level of a government deficit may be sustainable so long as the rate of growth of the economy exceeds the rate of interest in real terms. Of course, this also needs political stability derived from a social consensus about the longer term economic perspective, which in turn requires an uninterrupted increase in the quality of life of the average citizen. In part, however, fiscal responsibility also requires serious resource mobilization by the government mostly through direct taxes rather than choosing, time after time, the soft option of indirect taxes on necessities of life and relying upon deficit financing.

In this pursuit, the object of tax reforms should be to broaden the base for direct taxes so that a larger number of people are brought into the tax net, and to deepen the structure of direct taxation by increasing the average rate of tax as a proportion of income, not by raising tax rates but by reducing tax avoidance in the form of admissible deductions and by reducing tax evasion through better enforcement and compliance. In the aggregate, public finance will be in a sustainable state if out of every increase in income, the increase in tax revenues collected exceeds the increase in government expenditure. For example, if income increases by Rs 100, say from Rs 1,000 to Rs 1,100, then this 'marginal' increase of Rs 100 in income should yield an additional revenue to government in taxes, say Rs 40 (if that is the marginal tax rate). This increase in government revenue should exceed the increase in government expenditure which should, therefore, rise by less than Rs 40. The satisfaction of this criterion will ensure a steady strengthening of public finance over time, without squeezing dramatically the ability of the government to borrow and spend for productivity enhancing investment, and for raising social consumption levels continuously over time.

III. ILLUSIONS AND REALITIES

One of the basic problems of liberalization as it is being practised in India today, is that it is wrongly conceived even in terms of economic theory. The Finance Minister and his learned mandarins in the Ministry of Finance, many of whom learnt their practice of economics in the IMF or the World Bank, use a smoke screen of economic technicalities to sell illusions. They pretend, for example, that the government must practice austerity for increasing international confidence in the rupee and creating a comfortable foreign exchange reserves situation. They take pride in the fact that the rupee is already convertible on the current account (which means little restriction on imports of goods or services and travel abroad) and will soon be convertible on capital account (which means no restriction on acquisition or repatriation of assets by citizens and foreigners). However, as we have emphasized repeatedly, this is mostly irrelevant from the point of view of an average Indian. The reason is simple. It has little to do with the economic priorities of the common man or woman, who has to live with harsher realities of life in India.

Let us suppose that the confidence in the rupee is maintained, but at the cost of increasing poverty, unemployment and illiteracy; or at the cost of creating shortages in basic infrastructural facilities, say in power, roads or housing. In that case, it is an artificial illusion to maintain confidence in the rupee. Its artificiality is currently underlined by the fact that large portfolio investments attracted by an artificially high interest rate are needed to keep the show of a strong rupee going. If, for some reason, the interest rate is drastically reduced, or non-resident Indians and foreign institutional investors find an avenue of higher returns on their investment elsewhere in the global economy, the strength of the rupee would evaporate with or without liberalization. Something like this did happen in Mexico not so long ago. It could happen in India also.

Unlike the present government or the IMF, we do not believe in creating flimsy illusions about the strength of the rupee. Instead, it needs to slowly develop a genuine strength. And the fact that India has not yet been fully integrated into the global economic system represents an opportunity, for it can be used as a strength rather than mourned as a weakness. Countries which have become more fully integrated in the world monetary system can no longer have large government deficits or relatively low interest rates to encourage domestic investment, because of the overwhelming fear that such measures will lead to a speculative flight of capital against their currencies. India still has some room for manouevre, precisely because the rupee is not internationally accepted as a convertible currency. It is not, at least so far, what economists would call an international 'store of value'. This is why non-residents also keep their money denominated mostly in freely convertible dollars, which is an international store of value or wealth, through special deposits or facilities provided by the government.

Our basic difference with current government policies arises from our conviction that confidence in any currency, especially in the currency of a developing country like India, needs to be built up gradually through an improved economic performance which is sustained over time. This does not only mean increasing exports, on which liberalization rightly lays a lot of stress. It also means an overall economic performance which improves the quality of life of the average citizen. The latter would impart a degree of political stability which, in turn, is a main determinant of better international credit ratings and favourable perceptions on the part of multinational corporations. What is more, the eradication of poverty, the creation of employment, the improvement in the quality of life would be based on incomes and purchasing power in the hands of the people. This would increase the size of the market in India. More than anything else, direct foreign investment is attracted by the size of the home market at least insofar as large countries such as India and China are concerned. The size of India's home market is our immediate bargaining strength vis-a-vis the terms and conditions for investments by multinational corporations. It is not very intelligent economic management either to reduce all customs duties *unilaterally*, or to reduce the size of the Indian home market by compressing government spending in the name of austerity. Such policies rob the country of its main bargaining power against multinational corporations.

It also needs to be mentioned here that even if we manage to attract a significant volume of direct foreign investment initially, this will not solve the problem of sustaining a rising per capita income in the economy. By definition, increasing purchasing power requires rising labour productivity in the economy. For the economist, this means raising levels and rates of investment in the economy so that there is a continuous creation and upgradation of productive capacities. But, in the long term, there are two other requirements that are vital : the acquisition of technological and managerial capabilities, and the development of human resources through education.

India is among a handful of developing countries which has a wide range of sophisticated domestic industries and skilled manpower. This was an advantage created mostly by post-independence Indian planning. And this is a strength which we must consolidate. We have explained earlier that a continuous enhancement of technologial capabilities does not come automatically with direct foreign investment. The government must play an active role in terms of industrial policy and technology policy, especially by inducing the private sector to finance research and development so that it can make a transition from importation to innovation, from know-how to know-why, in the long run. Instead, the current government policy will hinder the development of domestic technological capabilities by accepting uncritically the international intellectual property rights regime. The inclination, it seems, is to run after multinational corporations as the source not only of technology but also of management. It is obvious that technologial and managerial capabilities will not be developed by waiting for non-resident Indians or multinational corporations.

Our higher education must begin to meet the challenge and contribute to the development of technological capabilities and managerial talents. It is for this reason that private funding of higher education should be encouraged, particularly in technical fields. Again, this will introduce some accountability in the higher education system. It should be made clear that we are not suggesting a substitution of government investment by private investment in higher education or technical education. We believe that the erosion of financial support for higher education from the government, in the name of structural adjustment, is a retrograde step. But we would also like to see additional private investment in the setting up of research institutions and universities of quality. Mindless populism has been one of the worst enemies of maintaining quality in higher education and generating meaningful research in India. A sense of vulgar populism in the guise of left rhetoric has been particularly responsible for downgrading the quality of higher education. Unless we wake up to this fact, and quickly, we must face the reality that international competitiveness, which rests on technological and managerial foundations, will continue to elude us, even if we dream of becoming global players. Those who talk of economic sovereignty must also realize that they cannot ride two horses at the same time: of populism in higher technical education and of opposing multinational corporations in political rhetoric. We must find a clear way of improving the quality of higher education, especially technical education, and funding it, so that we can achieve international competitiveness through the development of technological capabilities in not too distant a future. India is one of the few developing countries which can do it. And we must do it.

IV. DEMOCRACY AND DEVELOPMENT

The success or the failure of economic liberalization will be judged continuously by ordinary people in terms of the contribution it makes to the process of economic development, as reflected not in government statistics, but in the daily experience of people. As yet, liberalization has really nothing to show for itself in this respect. But economic development which concerns the life of ordinary people is far too serious a matter to be left only to economists, or even to politicians. It must be embedded in the feasible politics of broad social consensus in a democracy. And consensus in an open society, which has a relatively short time horizon of five years shaped by elections, can be achieved only when the economic system scrupulously maintains both transparency and accountability.

We would like to emphasize what we have said before. Transparency requires that the government must share information with the parliament, with the press and, above all, with the people. Accountability cannot be limited to corruption and immorality in public office. It also requires that individuals and institutions in the government are accountable for their actions in the discharge of public responsibilities. The reason is obvious. The people have a democratic right to know the basis of decisions made by the government, just as they have a democratic right to reward performance and penalize dishonesty, incompetence or negligence in the government. In a democracy, these principles of transparency and accountability must begin with the government but must be extended to political parties.

It is only such transparency, combined with accountability, that can ensure a long term commitment to economic development irrespective of election results in a political democracy. After objectives and policies, or strategy and tactics, are openly debated and accepted, political parties will be more or less obliged to honour their commitments on issues where a consensus has been reached irrespective of electoral successes and failures. Differences will remain. So will disagreements. But these must be in the open. Such differences or disagreements are just as important because they sustain the self-correcting mechanisms which are the essence of democracy. Let us illustrate this proposition with an example. There may be agreement between political parties on the provision of, say, drinking water or primary education. There may be disagreement between political parties on, say, foreign investment in the consumer goods sector. Transparency combined with debate, which highlights both the consensus and the dissensus, will give our economic policies the essential element of stability, where both continuity and change are an integral part of a long-term view. The present set of policies is not characterized by such stability because the government has been neither open nor transparent about economic liberalization. However, an open debate and a long term view which imparts stability to the system is essential for development.

As we have said, that our emphasis on transparency and accountability is not so much about morality in public life. Nor does it stem from a desire to preserve the letter, or even the spirit, of the constitution in political life. We attach so much importance to these principles because they provide the means of combining sensible economics with feasible politics in India. The economic priorities of the people will be reflected more and more in the political agenda of the parties if there is transparency in the system. And the political agenda of the parties will be reflected more and more in the reality of economic development if there is accountability in the system. Once this two-way process gathers momentum, transparency and accountability will create a commitment to long term objectives of development in the context of a political democracy where governments are bound to change through elections over time.

We recognize that transparency and accountability are necessary but cannot be sufficient to ensure that political democracy and economic development strengthen one another. We are also aware that transparency based on a free flow of information and accountability based on a fixing of responsibility will inevitably result in time-consuming debates and slower decision-making processes. We are only too conscious that the past five decades of democracy in India have experienced diminishing transparency and accountability. But there is reason for hope. For one, we are in transition from a one-party system to a multi-party system and from an era of majority politics to an era of coalition politics. This change, in itself, will be much more conducive to transparency and accountability. For another, as democracy has taken roots at the level of the people, there is not only an increasing political consciousness among voters but also an increasing participation in the political process combined with an emerging mobilization on some issues. Thus the demand for transparency and accountability will come from the people. The strengthening of these attributes in our political system could create a momentum of its own, if the democratic process which is slow but sure, begins to shape the politics and the economics of development.

Paradoxically enough, the apparent weaknesses may be the real strengths of democracy in the longer run. This is, in a sense, borne out by the experience of former planned economies of East Europe and the erstwhile Soviet Union. Although these countries maintained their long-term commitment to a particular future course of economic development, and some dimensions of their economic progress were impressive, they went hopelessly wrong without accountability and without a democratic device for self-correction. Market-oriented democracies won precisely on this ground. Thus self-correction in our democracy, even though relatively slow moving, could become our greatest strength. No enlightened dictatorship or ruling elite which claims to know better should be permitted to weaken this self-correcting character of a democracy. In a parallel vein, all arguments against transparency, against the right to information, and all attempts to evade accountability, on the part of those in public office, should be fought if liberalization is to proceed in a sensible way in a country of India's complexity.

Economic development embedded in the democratic politics of social consensus is neither a matter of technical economics nor a question of managing politics with temporary slogans and illusions. More than anything else, economic development in a democracy must be recognized as the creation of purposive social organization. This means people are at the centre of economic development not only as its beneficiaries but also as the main actors. Our ordinary citizens, men and women, are our greatest resource when economic development is viewed as the creation of a purposive social organization. However, that sense of purpose in society can come only when ordinary people are enthused with a sense of achievement and a widening of economic opportunity in their day to day existence. Unfortunately, liberalization has given that enthusiasm and the opportunity only to the privileged upper-middle-class Indians, but not to the vast poor majority. The 'secession of the successful' may be the outcome, as in Latin America. In the process, a narrow segment of our population may be integrated with the world economy, but a large proportion of our population may be marginalized even further in India. This is why austerity now for a brighter and distant future has been a political non-starter in India. It forgets that ordinary people must be responsible for ushering in development. They must be enthused with a sense of steadily improving well-being.

This is the main reason why we differ from standard recipes of economic liberalization because it has failed to create in India that sense of enthusiasm without which the purposive social organization for development cannot come into existence. This is the challenge facing us all. To meet this challenge, the role of both the State and the market must be redefined without blind faith in either. We must learn to attach the highest priority to the economic aspirations of the ordinary people, the common man, and redefine the role of institutions, whether the State or the market, from that point of view. The scope and the direction of genuine economic liberalization relevant for India will emerge only from such a redefinition, and not from the ideological glorification of either. Let that rethinking start here and now.

Select Bibliography

In our endeavour to be reader-friendly, we have departed from the academic convention of providing references to the literature, citing sources for statistical evidence and writing scholarly footnotes. It seemed to us that a text cluttered with references, sources and footnotes would only distract the reader. We thought that it would be preferable to put together a select bibliography at the end. For the convenience of interested readers, this is divided into two parts: *references* used in, or related to, the arguments developed in the book; and *sources* of statistical evidence presented, or other information provided, in the book.

References

Amsden, A.H., *Asia's Next Giant: South Korea and Late Industrialization*, Oxford University Press, New York, 1989.

Amsden, A.H., 'Why Isn't the Whole World Experimenting with the East Asian Model to Develop?', *World Development*, Volume 22, 1994, pp.627-634.

Avramovic, D. et.al., *Economic Growth and External Debt*, Johns Hopkins University Press, Baltimore, 1964.

Bhagwati, J. and Srinivasan, T.N., *Indian Economic Reforms*, Ministry of Finance, New Delhi, July 1993.

Bhalla, G.S. *ed., Economic Liberalization and Indian Agriculture*, ISID-FAO, New Delhi, 1994.

Chakravarty, S., *Development Planning: The Indian Experience*, Clarendon Press, Oxford, 1987.

Corbo, V., Goldstein, M. and Khan, M. *eds., Growth Oriented Adjustment Programs*, International Monetary Fund and The World Bank, Washington DC, 1987.

Cornia, G., Jolly, R. and Stewart, F., *Adjustment with a Human Face*, Clarendon Press, Oxford, 1987.

Cordoso, F.H., 'Dependency and Development in Latin America', *New Left Review*, No. 74, 1972, pp.83-95.

Bhaduri, A. and Steindl, J., 'The Rise of Monetarism as a Social Doctrine', *Thames Papers in Political Economy*, Autumn, 1983.

Bhaduri, A., 'Dependent and Self-reliant Growth with Foreign Borrowing', *Cambridge Journal of Economics*, vol. 11, 1987, pp.269-73 (reprinted in *Unconventional Economic Essays*,

The Intelligent Person's Guide to Liberalization

Selected Papers of Amit Bhaduri, Oxford University Press, Delhi, 1993).

Bhaduri, A. and Marglin, S.A., 'Unemployment and the Real Wage: The Economic Basis for Contesting Political Ideologies', *Cambridge Journal of Economics*, vol. 14, 1990, pp.375-93 (reprinted in *Unconventional Economic Essays*, op. cit.).

Bhaduri, A., 'Conventional Stabilization and the East European Transition' in S. Richter *ed. The Transition from Command to Market Economies in East-Central Europe*, Westview Press, San Francisco, 1992.

Dell, S., *On Being Grandmotherly: The Evolution of IMF Conditionality*, Princeton Essays in International Finance, No. 144, Princeton, October 1981.

Dell, S., 'Stabilization: The Political Economy of Overkill', *World Development*, vol. 10, 1982, pp.597-612.

Domar, E.D., 'The Effect of Foreign Investment on the Balance of Payments', *American Economic Review*, 1950.

Fukuyama, F., 'The End of History', *The National Interest,* vol. 16, 1989, pp. 3-18,

Friedman, M., 'A Theoretical Framework for Monetary Analysis', *Journal of Political Economy*, vol. 78, 1970, pp. 193-238.

Government of India, *The Current Economic Situation and Priority Areas for Action*, Report of the Economic Advisory

Council, New Delhi, December 1989.

Government of India, *Statement on Industrial Policy*, Ministry of Industry, New Delhi, 24 July 1991.

Government of India, *Statement on Trade Policy*, Ministry of Commerce, New Delhi, 13 August 1991.

Government of India, *Economic Reforms: Two Years After and the Task Ahead*, Ministry of Finance, New Delhi, June 1993.

Hicks, J.R., *Capital and Growth*, Clarendon Press, Oxford, 1965.

International Monetary Fund, *Theoretical Aspects of the Design of Fund-supported Adjustment Programmes*, IMF, Washington DC, September, 1987 (occasional paper 55).

International Monetary Fund, *The Monetary Approach to the Balance of Payments*, IMF, Washington DC, 1977.

Kaldor, N., 'Inflation and Recession in the World Economy', *Economic Journal*, vol. 86, 1976, pp.703-714.

Kaldor, N., 'The New Monetarism', *Lloyds Bank Review*, July 1970.

Kalecki, M., *Selected Essays on the Dynamics of the Capitalist Economy*, Cambridge University Press, Cambridge, 1971.

Keynes, J.M., *The General Theory of Employment, Interest and Money*, Macmillan, London, 1936.

Lall, S., *Building Industrial Competitiveness in Developing*

Countries, OECD Development Centre, Paris, 1990.

Lok Sabha Secretariat, *Report of the Joint Committee to Enquire into Irregularities in Securities and Banking Transactions*, Volumes I and II, New Delhi, December 1993.

Naipaul, V.S., *India: A Million Mutinies Now*, Heinemann, London, 1990.

Nayyar, D., 'Transnational Corporations and Manufactured Exports from Poor Countries', *Economic Journal*, vol. 88, 1978, pp.59-84.

Nayyar, D., 'Political Economy of International Trade in Services', *Cambridge Journal of Economics*, vol. 12, 1988, pp.279-298.

Nayyar, D., 'Macro Economics of Stabilization and Adjustment: The Indian Experience', *Economie Appliquee*, vol. 48, 1995, pp.5-37.

Nayyar, D., *Economic Liberalization in India: Analytics, Experience and Lessons*, Orient Longman, Calcutta, 1995.

Nayyar, D. and Sen, A., 'International Trade and the Agricultural Sector in India', in G.S. Bhalla *ed. Economic Liberalization and Indian Agriculture*, ISID- FAO, New Delhi, 1994.

Planning Commission, *Employment: Past Trends and Prospects for the 1990s*, Government of India, New Delhi, 1990.

Planning Commission, *Report of the Expert Group on Estimation of Proportion and Number of Poor*, Government of India, New Delhi, 1993.

Polak, J.J., 'Monetary analysis of income formation and payments problems', *IMF Staff Papers*, Washington DC, IMF, vol. 5, 1957, pp.1-50.

Pollard, S., 'Industrialization and the European economy', *Economic History Review*, 2nd series, vol. 26, 1973.

Polyani, K., *The Great Transformation*, Holt, Rinehart and Winston, New York, 1944.

Scott, J., *The Moral Economy of the Peasant*, Yale University Press, New Haven, 1976.

Shaw, G.B., *The Intelligent Woman's Guide to Socialism, Capitalism, Sovietism and Fascism* (first published, Medium, June 1928), Constable, London, 1949 (standard edition).

Singh, A., 'Openness and the Market Friendly Approach to Development: Learning the Right Lessons from Development Experience', *World Development*, vol. 10, pp. 1811-1824.

Solomon, R., 'A perspective on the debt of developing countries', *Brookings Papers on Economic Activity No. 1*, 1977.

Taylor, L., *Structuralist Macroeconomics*, Basic Books, New York, 1983.

Taylor, L., *Varieties of Stabilization Experience: Towards Sensible Macroeconomics in the Third World*, Clarendon Press, Oxford, 1988.

Thaler, R.H., *The Winner's Curse*, Chapter 14 (written in collaboration with K.A. Froot), Princeton University Press,

Princeton, 1992.

Wade, R., *Governing the Market*, Princeton University Press, Princeton, 1991.

Williamson, J., *ed., IMF Conditionality*, Institute of International Economics, Washington DC, 1983.

World Bank, *The East Asian Miracle: Economic Growth and Policy*, Washington DC, 1993.

Sources

Bank of International Settlements, *Survey of Foreign Exchange Market Activity*, Basle, 1990.

Central Statistical Organisation, *National Accounts Statistics*, New Delhi, annual.

Government of India, *Economic Survey*, Ministry of Finance, New Delhi, annual.

Government of India, *Export-Import Policy*, Ministry of Commerce, New Delhi, March 1990 and March 1992.

Government of India, *India's External Debt: A Status Report*, Ministry of Finance, New Delhi, October 1993.

Government of India, *Union Budget* documents, Ministry of Finance, New Delhi, annual.

International Monetary Fund, *World Economic Outlook*, Washington DC, annual.

Organisation for Economic Co-operation and Development (OECD), *Financial Market Trends*, Paris, various issues.

Reserve Bank of India, *Annual Report*, Bombay, various issues.

Reserve Bank of India, *Report on Currency and Finance*, Bombay, annual.

Reserve Bank of India, *Report of the Policy Group and Task Force on External Debt Statistics of India*, Bombay, 1992.

The Economist, London, various issues.

United Nations, *World Investment Report: Transnational Corporations and Integrated International Production*, New York, 1993.

United Nations Conference on Trade and Development (UNCTAD), *Trade and Development Report*, Geneva, annual.

World Bank, *World Development Report*, Washington DC, annual.

Index